FINDING
YOUR TRUTH

How to Discover the Real You and
What You Were Born to Do

MICHELE YEOMANS
&
MALA BRIDGELAL RAM

10-10-10 Publishing

FINDING YOUR TRUTH
How to Discover the Real You and What You Were Born to Do

First edition published by
Michele Yeomans & Mala Bridgelal Ram

www.findingyourtruthbook.com

ISBN: 978-1-5442-2772-6

DEDICATION

This book is dedicated to all those seeking
a greater truth and understanding
about themselves.

TABLE OF CONTENTS

Chapter 5: An introduction to the 9 Energetic Qualities

ACKNOWLEDGEMENTS

Our thanks go out to those who have helped in the creation of this book whether directly or indirectly.

To Marta Orlowska, Simone Stewart, Sirkka Richert, Tomasz Jankowski, Nandini Gosine and Giselle Pierre-Nichols for their unwavering support, constant encouragement and welcomed contributions.

To John Demartini, Roger Hamilton and Christopher Howard who inspired us through their teachings. They allowed us to step into our power, live a life of truth and realise our infinite potential.

To Keri Murphy, Catharine Watkins, Sophia Smith, David Nassim, Stewart Pearce, Amanda Kent and Hugh Milne, our mentors and coaches who have challenged us to continually move forward and provided us with the tools to broaden our knowledge.

To our expanding community for putting their continued trust in us to guide them towards finding their truth and stepping into what they were born to do.

To Raymond Aaron, our publisher, and Vishal Morjaria, our book architect. Through their guidance they have made this book a reality.

To all the authors in our extensive library collection. Their written words have opened our minds to new knowledge and possibilities so that we may pass it on to others.

And last but not least, to our families and friends for their continued unconditional love and support.

FOREWORD

By Raymond Aaron

'The two most important days in your life are the day you were born, and the day you find out why.'
—Mark Twain

Why did you pick up this book?

It could be that Mark Twain's words resonate with you, and you may have a desire to understand why you were born and what you were put on this earth to do.

Currently, there are only two ways that direct you to what you were born to do. The first is career guidance, which is fine unless you are trying to change your career. The second is spiritual guidance, which is very nurturing but rarely ever comes to a conclusion. What Mala and Michele have managed to do in this book is nothing short of incredible. By using deceptively simple exercises, you are able to effectively draw out your truth which has eluded you until now.

Finding Your Truth is a most insightful and inspirational experience. What you thought you knew about yourself will be turned on its head, as you are taken through a set of methodical exercises pinpointing your core essence and revealing or reiterating who you really are. The result is a sense of clarity and purpose, which empowers you to step into a life of truth, flow and fulfilment.

Prepare yourself for a series of powerful and life-changing self-discoveries!

INTRODUCTION

The Million Dollar Question

We all want to live authentic lives. But how can you be authentic if you don't know who you truly are?

Society and other influences

The truth of who you are is not as clear cut as you think. Your values and beliefs, born out of familial and societal influences, are so deeply rooted within you that you actually believe that this is you. You continue on this journey by default. But these values and beliefs may not be yours. You have absorbed them from your surroundings and, without question, you follow the masses. That is until one of the following happens: a) life throws you a curve ball, b) you start to ponder that 'there must be more to life than this' or c) you go on a spiritual quest for a deeper understanding. One or more of these may cause you to re-evaluate everything you believed about you and your life.

With this re-evaluation comes a very one-sided conclusion. You understand precisely what you don't want. However, it gets very foggy trying to figure out what it is that you do want. To try and lift this fog you look to see what others are doing. You then mimic these people, believing them to be happy, successful or fulfilled, thinking that if you do what they are doing you can have the same outcome. This tactic will have very limited success unless you happen to have the same personality, drive, skill set and experience of those you wish to mimic. The many courses in property, forex training and online marketing are prime examples of this. They claim if you just do what they say you will be a millionaire. And if we were to believe their claims we should all be millionaires by now. Sadly, we are not.

The route to fulfilment

The trend now is that people are coming away from a life they don't want to be living and are looking for direction. But there is very limited useful guidance available. Referring to the last paragraph, it becomes very apparent that what works for others will not necessarily work for you. So how do you determine what is right for you? You need to know yourself inside out. The more you know about yourself the easier it will be to make decisions and choices that are right for you. This is key if you are to lead a happy and fulfilled life. You need to reassess your values and beliefs that, up until now, have been limiting your potential. You will recognise these limiting factors because they immediately drain your energy. You may find yourself having to psych yourself up and put on a brave face simply to face the day ahead. All of this is an indication that you are not living an authentic life which is why you may feel life is a struggle or that you are not making any progress.

> The more you know about yourself the easier it will be to make decisions and choices that are right for you.

Think about the vast majority of people who are unhappy in their working life. Their beliefs are forcing them to stay in that job. These beliefs may include a) not being good enough for anything better, b) it is safer to stay in what you know than to take a risk on what you don't know or c) that their talents and expertise are limited only to the jobs they have previously done. Considering that we spend at least two-thirds of our lives working it is no wonder that the majority of the population is unhappy.

You are so much more than your job description. As soon as you start to look at yourself from a different perspective you begin to see greater opportunities, move beyond your fears and develop incredible personal power. And the good news is, once you are on this path you can achieve anything you put your mind to. Your mind expands, and an expanded mind can never go back to its original size.

> An expanded mind can never go back to its original size.

How do you begin to look at yourself from a different perspective? By understanding the underlying themes that drive your choices and actions. These underlying themes are usually hidden or go unrecognised, but they form the core and truth of who you are. This knowledge is key because the route to fulfilment is first understanding your truth and then ensuring whatever you chose to do in this lifetime is in alignment with that truth.

> The route to fulfilment is first understanding your truth

You can't afford not to

According to Bronnie Ware, the Australian author and palliative care nurse, the number one death bed regret is not living a life true to who you are (Ware, 2012). The vast majority of unhappy workers have settled for a life of mediocrity by not living their truth. You don't have to.

This book will help you to find your truth, understand who you are at your core and ultimately discover the work you were born to do. This is the start of your journey to self-actualisation.

But you must act now. Don't choose a repetitive, unfulfilled life. Embrace your truth and watch the magic happen.

Go to <u>www.findingyourtruthbook.com</u> to download three key bonus trainings to get you in the right mindset as you begin this journey.

CHAPTER 1

UNDERSTANDING THE JOURNEY

Your purpose vs the work you were born to do

People often get hung up or even obsessed about finding their purpose. This is driven by a desire for finding deeper meaning in their lives. They turn to astrology, numerology, psychics, tarot card readers and the like. However, the answers they receive may have that wow factor but they are usually presented as abstract ideals. They tend to be vague, generic descriptions and most people struggle to make practical use of this information. More often than not, you cannot even conceive how this will happen. So you continue your quest without any real progress. You are usually left with more questions than answers, especially around the area of how you can practically step into your purpose.

> The work you were born to do is a tangible way of achieving your purpose

The work you were born to do is a tangible way of achieving your purpose, whether you are aware of what your purpose is or not. In fact, when you step into what you were born to do, you will actively begin to live your purpose. So don't get hung up on finding your purpose, it will happen automatically. But, if you are still curious, Dan Millman's book *The Life You Were Born to Live* is a good starting point and a worthwhile read. However, as noted above it will only be general guidance.

This book, on the other hand, will give you clear and practical steps you can take towards discerning what you were born to do, allowing you to step into your purpose. You will understand yourself much more clearly and begin to see yourself in a new light. This enables you to see opportunities or avenues that you can pursue that you would perhaps not have considered before, allowing you to choose what is right for you. This creates new possibilities leading to a deep trust and realisation that you have a significant part to play in shaping humanity.

Experience not required

It may be that this is a new journey for you or perhaps you may have explored different avenues in an attempt to understand what you were born to do. On our journey we read books, attended courses, workshops and seminars, all of which contributed to our growth and development but still did not answer that burning question, 'What was I born to do?'

The more spiritual approach was very self-reflective but gave no clear direction and again left us with more questions than answers. The career approach, which is based on our previous work experience, took us back to our respective industries, and this was precisely what we were trying to get away from.

As it turned out, once we understood what we were born to do, we began to see the connections. We realised that what we gravitated towards, our approach to life and our internal thought processes, had been leading us to this point, although at the time it felt quite random.

The reality is the work you were born to do is an extension of your true self and once this is revealed you will be inspired to follow your true path.

The unseen always supports the seen

One of the laws that governs the universe is that the unseen always supports the seen. Think about this for a second. The roots of a tree are underground and unseen. However, without the roots there would be no tree. The foundation of a building is also underground and unseen but without it the building would soon collapse.

> One of the laws that governs the universe is that the unseen always supports the seen.

The stronger and more resilient the 'unseen', the stronger and more resilient the 'seen'. If the root of a tree is not being nourished, the tree will grow very weak and may eventually die. However, if it is well nourished it will grow to be strong and healthy.

Why is this important? Because this law exists in us all. If your 'unseen' (which is your thoughts, emotions, values and beliefs) is not strong nor supportive of your growth, then this will hinder or halt your progress. For example, take two work colleagues with exactly the same job title. One has confidence (unseen) whilst the other doesn't. The one with confidence will progress faster in the company than the one without.

Within each of us, there is an unseen root system that needs to be nurtured and nourished. This is crucial for our health, happiness and overall well-being. More importantly, it is the foundation for understanding what it is you were born to do.

Your personal root system

The more your personal root system is allowed to express itself, the better your quality of life and the happier you will be. What is your personal root system? Your personal root system is the core, unseen aspect of yourself which unconsciously

> The more your personal root system is allowed to express itself, the better your quality of life and the happier you will be.

drives your actions, behaviours and decisions. We have identified three specific areas in this system: your Inner Code™, your Inherent Nature™, and your Internal Process™.

Inner Code™

Your Inner Code™ is like a gravitational pull; you are always drawn to it. When it is present in your life you are at your happiest, and if it is absent you are very uncomfortable and unhappy. It is a very powerful tool, not only for decision-making but also for understanding what really drives your happiness.

Inherent Nature™

Your Inherent Nature™ is your unseen personality. It is the essence of who you are. Understanding your Inherent Nature™ gives genuine clarity to your approach to everyday life. When you work with your Inherent Nature™ your life will be in flow.

Internal Process™

Your Internal Process™ is the way your mind automatically creates a strategy for dealing with what is in front of it. Again, this is not visible to the naked eye and most times you are not even aware that it exists. You just do it automatically. This is the key to unlocking your genius.

How not to do it

The current trend for anyone looking for a more fulfilling job or career path is to start by finding what you are passionate about and pursuing that. However, we run into a few challenges here. First, not everyone is passionate about something. Certainly, when we started this journey there was nothing that we could identify that we were really passionate about. So that was a non-starter. But suppose you are at the opposite end of the scale and you have so many things you are passionate about. How do you choose one? And if by chance you do have something you are passionate about, does this necessarily infer that you have a natural talent for it? Evidence (especially if you follow the qualifying rounds of X-Factor or Britain's Got Talent) has shown that just because we are passionate about something does not necessarily mean we have a talent for it. Suppose you do have a talent for it and you follow it, does this guarantee that you will be happy? Probably not. Many follow their dream job only to be disillusioned and stressed by either the environment (e.g. office politics or personality clashes) or the industry (e.g. long working hours or fierce competition). All of which leads to a very unhappy workforce.

What now

Rather than starting the process with your passions, start by first understanding your unseen root system. This Inner Code™, Inherent Nature™ and Internal Process™ are key to understanding what needs to be in place for you to thrive. As long as your passions and talents are supported by your personal root system you will be happy with your chosen path.

This book will help you to clearly understand your personal root system. It is about you getting to know you. We start at the root and work our way up just as nature intended. Each chapter is carefully designed to help you uncover different aspects of yourself, which involves a lot of question-based, introspective work. The process is simple yet very powerful. Rather than coming away with more questions than answers, you will have greater clarity and direction.

How to use this book

For the most part, the chapters are structured first with learning points followed by exercises for you to complete. We suggest the following:

- Use a notebook specifically for recording your answers to all the exercises in this book.

- Create a 'Results Page'. This can be a page in your notebook or a separate page. Here you will record your answers and key points from all the exercises.

- Approach each chapter in chronological order as the chapters follow a logical sequence allowing you to discover who you are and what you were born to do.

- Take time to think through the answers. It could be that this style of questioning is new to you and will require inner reflection. Don't feel as if you have to rush but give them careful consideration and, if necessary, you may revisit and refine your answers at a later date.

- We have given examples to clarify our points. Our clients' names in these examples have been changed to protect their identity.

Before you start, here is a story to help you understand why you need to read this book!

Storytime

'There was a time, according to Hindu legend, when people had all the knowledge of the gods. Yet time and time again they were more interested in pleasures of the flesh than they were in using the wisdom that was lying at their feet. (Times haven't changed much, have they?) One day, a god called Brahma decided to hide this wisdom where only the most persistent would discover it. He was tired of openly giving the people a gift they weren't using. And he knew if humans had to look for the answer they would more wisely use it. "Let's bury it deep inside the Earth" one god suggested. Brahma replied, "No. Too many people will dig down into the Earth and find it." "Then let's put it in the deepest ocean" said another. Brahma rejected that idea too. "People will learn to dive and will find it someday" he said. A third god asked, "Why don't we hide it on the highest mountain?" To which Brahma replied, "No. People can climb the highest mountain. I have a better place. Let's hide it deep inside the people themselves. They will never think to look for it in there."

So it was - and so it is.'

—Author unknown.

We wish you every success on your journey.

CHAPTER 2

YOUR INNER CODES™

Introduction

Whenever we have mentioned the term Inner Codes™ to life coaches or anyone that has ever been coached, they automatically assume that their Inner Codes™ are the same as their values. This is incorrect. Although the list of the Inner Codes™ may look similar to values, they are not values. By definition, the term 'value' means something that is important to you. This means that you have made a conscious decision to aspire to those values and you can change them at any given time.

> Your Inner Codes™ are not a conscious choice. They chose you, you did not choose them.

Values come in two categories, living values and moral values. Living values tend to change as we get older; for example, in your teens you valued computer games and hanging out with friends. In your twenties, your values are career orientated. In your thirties, putting down roots is important to you, etc. Moral values are a set of principles that guide your behaviour and actions. They are deep-seated convictions that you hold, allowing you to distinguish your interpretation of right and wrong. Again, moral values may change over time.

Your Inner Codes™, on the other hand, are not a conscious choice. They chose you, you did not choose them. They have been with you since the day you were born with and will be with you until you die. Think of them from this perspective. A parent may have two young sons. The first may perhaps cling to his mother, possibly revealing that 'Security' could be one of his Inner Codes™. If this is one of his Inner Codes™, then he will exhibit this need for security throughout his life, although it will show up in different forms. The second son grabs the opportunity to run off at any given moment. It may be that 'Adventure' is one of his Inner Codes™. If this is truly one of his Inner Codes™, he will exhibit this need for 'Adventure' throughout his life, although it will show up in different forms. No one taught them this behaviour. They were just born that way. And this is the difference between values that are changeable and Inner Codes™ that are not. So let us now look at what really constitutes your Inner Codes™.

What are your Inner Codes™?

Your Inner Codes™ are key elements that, if present, mean you are okay with the world and your life is in flow. If they are not present you are unhappy, frustrated or uncomfortable. Most people do not realise that these Inner Codes™ exist but they are drawn to them like a magnet whenever they are present. It is almost akin to health in that when we have good health we don't think about it, but it's only when we are ill that we look for the cause. It is easier to see the signs with health issues, as our body usually alerts us to the problem. However, with Inner Codes™ there are no visible signs, and because you do not realise that they exist, you do not look for them.

When we are in a negative space we look for reasons as to why we feel this way and usually allocate blame to people and circumstances. However, this is only a symptom and just touches the surface of the problem. To really get to the root of your unhappiness or frustration you need to identify and understand your Inner Codes™, as these are the true indicators of why you feel the way you do, whether that is good or bad.

These Inner Codes™ show up in all areas of your life, not just in your career. They are very useful when you need to make key decisions in any aspect of your life.

> Your Inner Codes™ are the true indicators of why you feel the way you do, whether that is good or bad.

Key attributes of your Inner Codes™

- They are like a magnetic pull, you are always drawn to them
- When they are present in your life, you are at your happiest
- If they are absent or restricted, you are very uncomfortable and unhappy
- They are used as decision-making tools
- They show up in every area of your life
- They give you the underlying reasons as to why you feel the way you do
- They have been with you since they day you were born

Why is this important?

As mentioned in the earlier chapters, happiness is not guaranteed just because you are doing something that you love to do. However, happiness can be guaranteed if you do what you love to do, whilst ensuring your Inner Codes™ are not restricted in any way.

The first step on your journey will be to find your Inner Codes™. Following this we will then map your favourite activities back to your Inner Codes™, confirming that they are both in alignment.

Exercise: What are your Inner Codes™?

Before you begin this exercise it may be worthwhile to get familiar with the forms in Appendices 1-4. You can download the pdf versions of these forms at <u>www.findingyourtruthbook. com</u>

- List of Inner Codes™ (Appendix 1)

  This is a comprehensive list of the most used Inner Codes™. Have a quick scan so that you get familiar with them. You will be referring to these Inner Codes™ throughout the exercise.

- Key Areas and Transitions in Your Life (Appendix 2)

  This document helps you to broaden your thinking as it guides you to look at your life in its entirety.

- Inner Codes™ Grid (Appendix 3)

  You will be completing this form as you go through this exercise. Included here is the full list of the Inner Codes™, Columns numbered 1 to 8 and finally a Total Column.

- Top 5 Inners Codes (Appendix 4)

  Once you have ascertained your top 5 Inner Codes™, you can transfer them here. You can then refer back to this for future reference.

Guidelines to uncovering your Inner Codes™

1. **The meaning of the words is whatever it means to you.**

   There is no right or wrong. In our workshops we usually ask our attendees to define the meaning of common words used in everyday language like 'love', 'work' or 'wealth'. Without fail, no two people ever have the same exact answer. The meaning is whatever it means to you because it brings your truth and your thinking to life. For example, our client Susan's definition of 'Connection' is connecting to other people whilst Mala's meaning of 'Connection' is the inter-connectedness of everything in the universe. Same word, very different meanings, but both reflect the key drivers of the individuals.

2. **If there are two words that mean the same thing to you, then cross off one and use the other.**

   It may be that two words will have a similar definition to you. For example, 'Independence' and 'Freedom'. To one person, 'Freedom' may encompass all aspects of life, whereas 'Independence' may simply mean the ability to do things on their own. However, if you think they both mean the same thing then, by all means, use only one. So please read through the list of Inner Codes™ (Appendix 1) and if there are two words that hold the same meaning for you, cross one of them off, both in Appendix 1 and Appendix 3 (Inner Codes™ Grid).

3. **As far as is possible or relevant, connect to your emotions when doing this exercise.**

   As you look for your answers, connect emotionally where required, which means going back to the memory and feeling what you were feeling back then. Emotions are key to understanding what was happening at that point in time. This will allow a more accurate representation of your Inner Codes™.

4. **Think sequentially and cover all aspects of your life.**

   We have a tendency to focus on what is currently going on in our lives and forget the past which may hold vital clues to the work you were born to do.

Appendix 2 comes in very handy here, to help you to cover all aspects of your life both horizontally (the eight primary areas) and vertically (the chronological sequence of your life).

5. **Be honest with yourself.**

Do not answer what you think you should be experiencing, but rather what you are really experiencing, even if it feels uncomfortable to you. This is all about you and if you believe you 'should' be experiencing something else, it is because you have not accepted who you are and you are looking outside yourself for who you would prefer to be. You are not owning or living your truth. One of our coaching clients, Mary, did this exercise originally and came up with 'Security' as one of her Inner Codes™. She did not like 'Security' because she preferred to be a risk taker like some of her friends. But when asked how she would feel if she had to leave her job without a backup plan (like one of her friends did) she was mortified and knew she would be totally stressed! Which just re-emphasised that 'Security' was one of her Inner Codes™. Once she understood this, she embraced it and left 'Security' as one of the top Inner Codes™.

6. **You are only looking for the top 5 Inner Codes™.**

We all have many Inner Codes™ and this will be evident as you go through the exercise. But some of those codes will be much more important to you than others. So you are looking for the top 5 Inner Codes™ which are your key drivers and will have the most influence in your life.

The exercise that you are about to do is wonderfully simple in its approach, yet still manages to get to the core of the matter.

Exercise: Uncovering your Inner Codes™

Step 1

Think of a time in your life when you were really, really happy. Your life was full of joy, ease and flow, and you felt like you were on top of the world. You might have been happy on more than one occasion but choose only one, the absolute happiest.

It can be a day, a week, a year, an event or a moment in time. Remember to look at all areas of your life and think sequentially (Appendix 2) to find that perfect time of happiness.

Connect emotionally with it. Begin by closing your eyes if you need to. Go back to that time and see what you saw, hear what you heard and really reconnect with those feelings. Be aware of everything that was happening to you at that time.

When you are ready do the following:

- Write about it and be as descriptive as possible

- Highlight or underline any words or phrases that link to an Inner Code™ (Appendix 1) that **were present** at that time and, because they were present, you were happy

- Then, in column 1 of the Inner Codes™ Grid (Appendix 3), tick only the ten most significant codes that you highlighted or underlined that were present.

Step 2

Think of a time when things were not going well. You were at your absolute worse. You felt stuck, trapped and frustrated, really unhappy. You might have been unhappy on more than one occasion but choose only one, the absolute worst.

It can be a day, a week, or a year, an event or a moment in time. Remember to look at all areas of your life and think sequentially (Appendix 2) to remember that time of unhappiness.

Connect emotionally with it. Begin by closing your eyes if you need to. Go back to that time and see what you saw, hear what you heard and really reconnect with those feelings. Be aware of everything that was happening to you at that time.

When you are ready do the following:

- Write about it and be as descriptive as possible

- Highlight or underline any words or phrases that link to an Inner Code™ (Appendix 1) that were **absent** at that time and, because they were absent, you were very unhappy. This time we are looking for things that were missing. And because it was missing it made you really unhappy.

- Then in column 2 of the Inner Codes™ Grid (Appendix 3), tick only the ten most significant codes that you highlighted or underlined that were not present or were missing

Step 3

Look at the following statement

'When I have _____ I feel at peace and in harmony with myself and the world around me.'

Looking at the list of Inner Codes™ in Appendix 1, choose the ten most appropriate words that you feel fit the statement above. Example: 'When I have "FREEDOM" I feel at peace and in harmony with myself and the world around me.' For all ten, say the sentence out loud so that it rings true for you and it feels right when you say it. If any of them does not feel right, then choose an alternative until you are comfortable with your choices.

Then in column 3 of your Inner Codes™ Grid (Appendix 3), select the ten words that you chose.

Step 4

Look at the following statement

'Without _____ I feel totally lost and hopeless.'

Looking at the list of Inner Codes™ in Appendix 1, choose the ten most appropriate words that you feel fit the statement above. Example: 'Without "FREEDOM" I feel totally lost and hopeless.' For all ten, say the sentence out loud so that it rings true for you and it feels right when you say it. If any of them does not feel right, then choose an alternative until you are comfortable with your choices.

Then in column 4 of your Inner Codes™ Grid (Appendix 3), select the ten words that you chose.

Step 5

If you were an animal which animal would you be?
It can be any animal that is:

- In existence (from field mouse to whale)
- Extinct (e.g. dinosaur, dodo, woolly mammoth)
- Mythical (e.g. dragon, unicorn, centaur)

Write down all the traits and characteristics that you admire in that animal and the reasons that you are drawn to that particular animal.

Then in column 5 of your Inner Codes™ Grid (Appendix 3), select the ten most significant Inner Codes™ that relate to the traits of that animal, as far as you can see a connection.

Step 6

You were just granted your perfect day (24 hours). Whatever you want for that day, it is yours. Assume money is no object and that you have no prior engagements or responsibilities.

Write descriptively about your day as if you were experiencing it now; who is there with you? What are you doing and how are you feeling? Connect emotionally with this perfect day.

Once you have done this, highlight or underline any words or phrases that link to an Inner Code™ (Appendix 1) that were present at that time on this perfect day.

Then as far as is possible, in column 6 of your Inner Codes™ Grid (Appendix 3), based on what you highlighted or underlined, select the ten most significant Inner Codes™ in so far as it relates to what you were feeling on that perfect day.

Step 7

What is your favourite book? It can be fiction or non-fiction. Choose only one.

What do you love about it? If it is fiction, what do you love about the characters, the scenes, the storyline, etc.? If it is non-fiction, what did you love about the topic, the content or the author?

Then write descriptively about the reasons you are drawn to the book.

Highlight or underline any words or phrases that link to an Inner Code™ (Appendix 1) that are present in the reasons you were drawn to the book.

As far as is possible, in column 7 of your Inner Codes™ Grid (Appendix 3), based on what you highlighted or underlined, select the ten most significant Inner Codes™ that are present in the aspects of what you loved about the book.

Step 8

Name your favourite film OR TV show/series. It cannot be the same as your favourite book in Step 7. If it is the same as your book, then choose your second favourite film or TV show/series.

What do you love about it? If it is fiction, what do you love about the characters, the scenes, the storyline, etc.? If it is non-fiction, e.g. documentary, what did you love about the topic, the content or the presenter?

Then write descriptively about the reasons you are drawn to the film or TV show/series.

Highlight or underline any words or phrases that link to an Inner Code™ (Appendix 1) that are present in the reasons you were drawn to the film or TV show/series.

As far as is possible, in column 8 of your Inner Codes™ Grid (Appendix 3), based on what you highlighted or underlined, select the ten most significant Inner Codes™ that are present in the aspects of what you loved about the film or TV show/series.

Step 9

Looking at your results.

Look at your results on your Inner Codes™ Grid (Appendix 3). For each Inner Code™ listed, you are now going to add the number of ticks across the page that you have assigned in columns 1 to 8 and put this total number in the Total Column.

Look down the Total Column and choose the 5 Inner Codes™ with the highest numbers. This becomes your top 5 Inner Codes™. You need both a clear, highest winner (i.e. no ties) and four additional numbers. Think about this like a dining room table: the clear highest winner is the table-top and the four additional numbers are the legs of the table, supporting the table-top.

If your top five numbers are a) all different and b) higher than all the other numbers, then great, you have no further work. Example: your top five may be 8,7,6,4,3, and all the other numbers are 1s or 2s.

If your top five numbers include a tie and if the tie is the two highest numbers then you will need to do the tie-breaker exercise as specified below. This is to determine your highest Inner Code™. If the tie is not in relation to the top place, then you don't need to do any further work. Example: your top five may be 8,8,7,6,4, in which case your two top numbers tie so you need to do the tie-breaker exercise. However, if your top five numbers are 8,7,7,6,4, and these are all higher than your other numbers, then no additional work is required.

If there is a tie for your fifth number, then you will also need to do the tie-breaker exercise. Example: if your top four numbers are 8,7,6,4, and the next highest is 3 which occurs more than once, then you need to do the tie-breaker exercise specified below to determine which Inner Code™ will become number five.

If your top five numbers include a tie and if the tie is neither for the first nor the fifth number, then no further work is required. Example: if your top five numbers are 8,7,7,5,4, and the other numbers are 3s and 2s, then no further work is required as the tie is in the middle.

Additional examples:

First five highest numbers	Next two highest numbers	What next?
7,6,5,4,3	2,1	Nothing.
7,6,5,5,4	3,2	Nothing.
8,8,6,6,4	3,2	Tie-breaker for first place only
8,6,5,5,4	4,3	Tie-breaker for fifth place only
7,7,6,4,4	4,4	Tie-breaker to be done for both first and fifth place

Dealing with ties

We are after the top 5 Inner Codes™. There must be a clear winner and four supporting Inner Codes™.

If there is a tie, then ask yourself the following question by filling in the blanks with the Inner Codes™ that are assigned the same value.

'If I could have _____ or _____ but not both,
I would have _____.'

Try not to over-think this. Repeat the question in your mind or out loud and let the answer instinctively and intuitively come out.

Example: if your Inner Codes™ of 'Freedom' tied with 'Trust', then you would ask yourself this question: 'If I could have 'Freedom' or 'Trust' but not both, I would have ….' The answer to this question will be the winner of the tie-breaker.

If your ties consist of three or more Inner Codes™ with the same value, then you need to look at all the possible pairings and do the tie breaker as above for each of the pairs and use the process of elimination until you have a clear winner.

Once you have completed this exercise and ascertained your top 5 Inner Codes™, then transfer this information to the Top 5 Inner Codes™ form in Appendix 4.

Step 10

Testing Your Inner Codes™

Having transferred your information onto the top 5 Inner Codes™ form, take a look at it and see if it resonates with you. Everyone has a different reaction when they first see their top 5 Inner Codes™. For some it can be a wonderful light bulb moment. Others may need time to process and ponder on what this means for them. How you connect with your Inner Codes™ really depends on how far along on your journey you are and how well you know yourself.

Hopefully you have answered the questions to the best of your ability and you are satisfied with the outcome. So now it is time to test if these are truly your top 5 Inner Codes™.

1. **Think back to a time when your life was in flow.**

    If these are truly your top five Inner Codes™ then you would notice that they were present and allowed to express themselves without restriction.

2. **Think back to a time when your life was not in flow.**

    If these are truly your top five Inner Codes™ then you would notice that they were severely restricted or absent for a long time. This creates strong emotions such as anger or frustration and at the first given opportunity you will do something to express or experience your Inner Codes™.

3. **Think back to your everyday life and childhood.**

    Your Inner Codes™ permeate all areas of your life and have been present since the day you were born. Think back to instances, both good and bad, in your childhood and in all areas of your life using points 1 and 2 above to test.

Your Top 5 Inner Codes™

You can now refer to this form at any time, as these Inner Codes™ are the first part of your personal root system. If one or more of your Inner Codes™ are severely restricted and/or absent for a long time, you will find that you are unhappy, almost to the point of suffering.

However, if there is no restriction towards living and experiencing your Inner Codes™ your life will be in flow. This does not mean that you live it 100% all the time, but more that it is available to you without restriction. For example, if 'Nurture' is one of your Inner Codes™ there is something in your life that you need to nurture, be it a person, career or cause. Although this may not be a full-time task, the fact that it is present in your life and you have access to it at all times means that you are in flow. However, if there is nothing for you to focus your nurturing energy on, your life may seem empty and without purpose, causing unhappiness.

> If there is no restriction towards living and experiencing your Inner Codes™ your life will be in flow.

But most times you are unaware that the true reason for this restlessness is that your Inner Code™ of nurturing is not allowed to express itself.

Use these Inner Codes™ as a decision-making tool. You should always choose the option that allows maximum expression of your Inner Codes™.

As indicated before, your Inner Codes™ are evident in all areas of your life. So be aware of the different areas they are showing up and the form in which they take. For example, one of Michele's Inner Codes™ is 'Clarity', and this is represented in clarity in understanding what it is she was born to do straight through to very clear labelling of anything she puts into the freezer. 'Clarity' shows up in all aspects of her life. So have an awareness of your Inner Codes™ and see how they are showing up in all the different areas of your life so that you can begin to own it and use it to your advantage.

Your 5 Inner Codes™ would have been present in your childhood and throughout your life.

If you are unable to see these 5 Inner Codes™ in both your past and present life, then you may need to re-do this exercise. The objective is that you should be able to see them in your day to day actions and truly connect with them.

Once you have connected to your top 5 Inner Codes™, transfer them to your 'Results Page' in whatever format you feel comfortable with. We will continue to build on the 'Results Page' as you progress through the book.

Final Words

Now that you are aware of your top 5 Inner Codes™ we will progress to the next chapter which will help you to shortlist the activities you are drawn to, by referring them back to your Inner Codes™.

CHAPTER 3

SHORTLISTING THE ACTIVITIES YOU ARE DRAWN TO

Debunking the myth

There are many books and courses developed that entice people with messages along the lines of: 'Make money from what you love doing', 'Follow your passion to find happiness' or 'Design your destiny'. The list goes on. This sounds simple enough but let's look at the following scenarios.

a. Unless you know that one thing that you are passionate about, it becomes difficult to make any progress.

b. Even if you know that one thing you are passionate about, there is no guarantee that you will be happy or successful following that path. In Michele's role as an accountant, she came across many individuals who followed their passion but ended up unhappy or disillusioned, eventually closing their business to follow another path.

c. It could be that you have too many things you are passionate about. This poses the problem of knowing which one of your many passions you should pursue. You may be afraid to move forward because you are scared of making the wrong choice, or if you do move forward it becomes a potentially lengthy and costly trial and error process.

d. You may have no idea what you are passionate about. In this instance, what happens is that you remain stuck because you don't know which direction to move in and because of this you may end up following the latest fad that promises freedom and wealth. Prime examples are online marketing, laptop lifestyle and property investment.

e. What if the word passionate is not in your vocabulary when it comes to describing a hobby or interest? It could be that you are interested in a few things but not overly excited or enthusiastic about any of them. This is where we found ourselves. Through the many self-development courses or the 'Find your destiny' type of courses, we always found ourselves limited in being able to follow their guidance simply because there was nothing that we could say that we were overly passionate about.

The courses out there are incomplete. Following your passion seems to be their main focus. However, following your passion may or may not give you the direction you are looking for. In addition, the courses do not take into account your Personal Root System or who you are as a person. This is the critical factor. Following your passion without your personal root system is like building a house (you are not even sure you want) without any foundation.

> Following your passion without your personal root system is like building a house without any foundation.

In our experience, we have found that it is not only about

your passions. What must be included here are those things that you may not consider to be one of your passions, but that you are nevertheless curious about and turn to routinely and consistently. Crucially, whatever you were born to do must be supported by your Inner Codes™. This guarantees that whatever you choose to do you will be happy, whether you are passionate about it or merely interested in it.

The following exercise is designed to take into account the two points made in the previous paragraph. Firstly, we will explore not just what you are passionate about but everything you gravitate towards. It is your everyday activities that will guide you to what you were born to do. Secondly, you will then map your

> It is your everyday activities that will guide you to what you were born to do.

Inner Codes™ to these activities. The activities that correlate to your top 5 Inner Codes™ will form a shortlist of potential areas you can begin to explore.

Please follow the guidelines carefully, particularly if you think you know what you were born to do and are just seeking confirmation. In our workshops, more often than not, attendees in that position usually emerge with a completely different direction.

Exercise: Shortlisting the activities you are drawn to

For this exercise, you will be using the form in Appendix 5 and referring to the form in Appendix 2. You can download the pdf versions of these forms at www.findingyourtruthbook.com

- *Activities you are drawn to* (Appendix 5)

    This form will be used to list and categorise all the activities that you are drawn to, including but not limited to your passions, interests and hobbies

- *Key Areas and transitions in your life* (Appendix 2)

  This document will help you to broaden your thinking as it guides you to look at your life in its entirety

Guidelines to finding the activities you are drawn to

1. **Have an open mind and let your answers flow.**

   If you have an idea of what you were born to do then pay particular attention to this guideline. Try not to let your current thinking influence your answers, otherwise this will taint the outcome. Approach each question objectively and intuitively to get the most out of this exercise.

2. **As far as possible, try not to duplicate your answers.**

   You may find that you have the same response to a number of questions. In this case, you only need to record it once. This will save you time later on when you need to do further work on your answers.

3. **Be concise; use single words or as few words as possible.**

   We strongly suggest that you use single words such as yoga, writing, dancing, etc. If required, use three words at most. Columns 2-4 will dig deeper into these answers and take considerably longer if your answers in column 1 are lengthy.

4. **Think sequentially and cover all aspects of your life.**

   We have a tendency to focus on what is currently

going on in our lives and forget the past, which may hold vital clues to the work you were born to do. Appendix 2, 'Key Areas and Transitions in Your Life', comes in very handy here, helping you to cover all aspects of your life both horizontally (the eight primary areas) and *vertically* (the chronological sequence of your life).

5. **Include everything you can think of.**

    Don't dismiss anything regardless of how bizarre it might appear to you or others. You are unique and, as such, what you were born to do will also be unique.

6. **Answer all the questions to the best of your ability.**

    The quality of the outcome of this exercise is directly proportional to the quality of your input. This means the more engaged and committed you are, the better the results. Superficial engagement equals superficial results. Give 100%.

7. **Assume that money, time and energy are unlimited.**

    Most of the time we refrain from things we would like to do because we think that money, time or energy is lacking. For this exercise assume these things are unlimited. This will bring to the forefront ideas that you might have previously dismissed.

8. **Use as many sheets (Appendix 5) as you need.**

    Don't limit yourself because you think you are writing too many activities. In fact, it is better to write too much rather than too little. These answers will eventually be shortlisted so write as many activities as you can think of. But remember point 2, try to avoid duplications.

9. **Answer as many questions as you can.**

   The exercise is based on a series of questions that are designed to help you to dig deeper, think broader and draw out the relevant information. You may not have answers to all the questions but try to answer as many of them as possible.

Step 1

Finding the activities you are drawn to

Record your answers in **Column 1 ONLY**. If you have more than one answer to any question, record each answer on a separate line in **Column 1**. For example, the question 'What do you do for relaxation?' may have more than one response like reading, watching TV, running, etc. Each of these responses will go into a line in **Column 1**. For example, 'reading' will go into one line, 'watching TV' into the line below and 'running' into the line below that one. Please leave Columns 2-4 blank as they will be used in a later part of the exercise.

With that in mind, please answer the following questions.

1. **What do you do for relaxation, pleasure or as a hobby?**

   This can be anything from the quiet to the more energetic activities. Think back throughout your life to uncover the things you did before time, money and responsibilities became an issue.

2. **What courses have you taken that you enjoyed?**

   Were there any courses that you took purely because they were of interest to you? Perhaps it was related to your job or business but nevertheless you really enjoyed it.

3. **What do you fill your personal space with?**

   Your personal space is anywhere that you are free to place items that are important to you. Example: your home, office, desk, living room, etc. What do you fill these places with? Books, plants, photographs?

4. **If you went into a mall which had every conceivable type of shop but you could only go into three, which three shops would you choose?**

   Here you are shopping for pleasure rather than necessity. Which shops would you make a beeline towards? Choose your top three. You may also include any shop that exists only in your imagination and has not yet made it to this earthly plane.

5. **What grabs your attention?**

   Is there anything that you are immediately drawn to, even if you just catch a glimpse of it? It could be things like an advertisement in the newspaper, a book title or something on social media that makes you curious enough to want to explore it further.

6. **What activities cause you to lose track of time?**

   Are there any activities that keep you so focused and engaged that when you look up at the clock you can't believe how much time has passed?

7. **What do you spend your money on that is not a necessity?**

   Is there anything that you buy just because you have to have it? Or anything that you buy on impulse? You may throw caution to the wind when it comes to buying these items.

8. **What do you speak to others about that gets you excited?**

   Are there any topics that you can talk at length about that really get you engaged and animated?

9. **What conversations or topics are you drawn to?**

   Have you ever eavesdropped or joined a conversation because what they were speaking about was so interesting and engaging?

10. **What do you strongly believe in or connect with?**

    Is there something that you connect with? It may be spiritual, political, social, environmental or universal.

11. **If you had to teach something, what would it be?**

    This will be a topic that really interests you. You may already be having conversations with others about this topic. Alternatively, you may be having your own internal dialogue or visualise yourself speaking to others about it.

12. **What are the three top things you wanted to do that you never got around to doing?**

    Is there anything that you ever wanted to do that, for one reason or another, you never managed to? You may also include anything that is not yet a physical possibility because current technology or knowledge does not yet support it. For an extreme example, time travel was listed by one of our workshop attendees.

13. **If you were to go into a bookstore or library for leisure, which section would you go to first?**

    Again, this bookstore or library (physical or digital) contains every conceivable topic or title. Which section or area would you immediately gravitate towards?

14. **What is your favourite field of interest, or what do you have a lot of knowledge on?**

Are there specific areas or topics where you have been accumulating knowledge? If you have been dipping into this field of interest over a long period of time you may be surprised at how much knowledge you have under your belt.

15. **What are you really curious about?**

When this topic is presented to you, your natural instinct is to find out more. You are not satisfied with the limited information provided. You want to go deeper. You may do your own research, ask other people or attend a course to gain more knowledge.

16. **Finally, retrace your steps over a weekend to see if there is anything you may have missed.**

Recall one of your typical weekends and notice in detail all the activities you were doing. This cognitive journey will help you to pick up on anything that you may not have thought of in the previous questions. If your weekend is not routine then choose any random weekend. These are activities you would do outside of your job or business, assuming that you have the freedom to do whatever you wish.

Step 2

Checking the feasibility of your answers

Whilst your answers may contain a comprehensive list of activities that you are drawn to, you may want to do a reality check to ensure that your activities are achievable and in alignment with who you are.

Consider the following and take action if required:

1. Look at your list for any activity that it is going to take you an incredibly long time to master. For instance, training to become a top class musician, brain surgeon or astronaut. If you are willing to put in the time and effort then, by all means, leave it in. However, if you feel that you cannot dedicate time to that pursuit then cross it off the list. For example, the attendee that had time travel on his list reluctantly crossed it off as he did not think it was achievable in his lifetime.

2. Look for any activity for which the only reason you have included it is to get away from someone or something. Hopefully you should not have any of these, but if you do please cross them off your list. The problem you face here is that you are unlikely to stick with it because the driving factor is not from you but related to something that is outside of you. Motivation must come from within.

3. Have a final check to ensure there are no duplicates.

Step 3

Getting more specific

You should now have a comprehensive list of activities you are drawn to. The next step is to dig deeper into those activities.

Using **Column 2**, identify the sub-categories for each activity listed in column 1. What you need to do here is be more specific about the type of activity you are drawn to. The best way to approach this is to ask yourself 'What type of _____ do I like?'

For example, if you put 'Books' in column 1 then ask yourself 'What types of books do I like?' Then in column 2 you will record the specific types of books you like to read. For example, Autobiographies, Personal Development, Spiritual, etc.

Alternatively, if one of your activities was 'Watching TV' in column 1, then in column 2 you need to write the type of programmes you like to watch. For example, Crime Dramas, Documentaries, Sports, etc.

Record as many sub-categories that you can think of and be as specific as possible. It may be that the activity in column 1 is already very specific and cannot be sub-categorised further. In this case, just transfer that activity to column 2. Example: if you put 'Hatha Yoga' as an activity in column 1, this is a very specific type of yoga that you will then record in column 2.

Step 4

Why are you drawn to these activities?

In this part of the exercise, you will examine the underlying reasons you are attracted to these activities. Although we are drawn to certain activities, very rarely do we take the time to understand why. We normally accept it without a second thought.

For each sub-category in column 2, you are now going to look behind the activity to discern the reason you were drawn to it and connect with what you were experiencing at that time. Record this in **Column 3**. As far as possible, put your experience into words to capture the feeling. The easiest way to do this is to consider the answers to the following questions:

- Why do I like to _____?
- What is it about _____ that draws me towards it?
- What am I gaining from _____?

For example, you may love to watch TV and movies, which you recorded in column 1. In column 2, one of the sub-categories may have been comedies. You now want to ask yourself the three questions noted above, inserting the sub-category into the blank space:

Why do I like comedies?

What is it about comedies that draws me towards them?

What am I gaining from comedies?

The answer may be that they make you laugh, they immediately lighten your mood or they may give you ideas for your own jokes. These answers will be recorded in column 3.

Or another example, you may have put 'Horse riding' in column 1. In column 2 you may have put 'Horse riding for leisure' and for column 3 ask yourself the following questions:

Why do I like horse riding?

What is it about horse riding that draws me towards it?

What am I gaining from horse riding?

The answer may be that you love being out in nature, having a sense of freedom or simply connecting with horses. Again, these are the answers you will record in column 3.

As you go through this exercise you will come up with reasons why you are drawn to these activities. Different activities may highlight the same or similar reasons. Although they may come from completely different sources, they are all linked to your underlying reasons.

Step 5

Mapping your answers to your Inner Codes™

In this part of the exercise you will begin to realise that everything you are drawn to is linked to your Inner Codes™. This is not necessarily just your top 5 Inner Codes™ that you ascertained in the previous chapter, but any of the Inner Codes™ that you assigned a value to.

For this exercise you will need your list of Inner Codes™ that you derived **before** you shortlisted them to the top five i.e. the full list that is in the total column of Appendix 3 on the work you did in chapter 2.

Looking at each answer you have given in column 3, match and record in column 4 the most appropriate Inner Code™ from the list described above that best suits it.

Continuing with the previous example of watching TV, these are the possible answers: TV (column 1)/comedies (column 2)/ Make you laugh (column 3). So in column 4 you may record 'Fun' or 'Humour' if this was included as one of your Inner Codes™. Remember, 'Fun' does not have to be one of your top 5 Inner Codes™.

And following the example with horse riding, these are the possible answers: Horse riding (column 1)/Horse riding for leisure (column 2)/Out in nature (column 3). So in column 4 you may record 'Nature' or 'Freedom' as your Inner Code™. Remember, this does not necessarily have to be one of your top five.

Once you have completed this exercise you will soon realise that all of the activities that you are drawn to will align with and support your Inner Codes™. The next step will be to identify which activities align and support our top 5 Inner Codes™.

Step 6

Shortlisting the activities you are drawn to

This is the final bit of the exercise where you identify the activities that have the most relevance for you.

Complete these final instructions:

1. **Look at <u>Column 4</u> and identify the rows that contain three or more of your top 5 Inner Codes™.** For these rows that you have identified, highlight the activities in **Column 2**. These activities will form the shortlist that will guide you towards the work you were born to do.

2. **Look at <u>Columns 1-4</u> for any words or themes that occur a few times and highlight them.** You are not looking for the activity here, but the words or themes that appear at least three times or more. These are indicative of an area that you need to investigate further and will lead you in the right direction.

3. **Finally, record the following on your 'Results Page'**

   a. Shortlisted activities from column 2

   b. Common words or themes from point 2 above.

Congratulations! You are starting to find your truth and as you progress through the book you will continue to build a profile of your Personal Root System and get to know the real you.

CHAPTER 4

YOUR INHERENT NATURE™

Introduction

As mentioned previously, there are things about us that may change over time such as our living and moral values. But there are other things that are such an inherent part of who we are that they will not change over time. We have already examined our Inner Codes™ which are with us from birth to death. Now we are going to explore our Inherent Nature™, which forms the second part of our Personal Root System.

In this and the next chapter we are going to cover:

- Traits
- Personalities
- Introverts and extroverts
- Preferred Representational System
- The 9 Energetic Qualities

… all of which will help to uncover even more about the truth of who you are.

Traits

What is a trait? A trait is a distinguishing quality or characteristic of an individual that can be either positive or negative. There are thousands of traits known to man and we each possess them all. We often perceive some traits to be missing, but the reality is that all of these traits are within us and available to us. The reason you do not see them all is because most of them are dormant,

> We often perceive some traits to be missing, but the reality is that all of these traits are within us and available to us.

so they don't manifest or show up in your day to day life. If you have ever said to yourself, 'Oh my god, I didn't know I had it in me?', that is when you are accessing a trait that was previously dormant but brought to life because you needed it at the time.

So when the time or the situation is right, you can access any dormant trait. For example, if you are a parent and your child is pinned under a heavy object, the parent may well gain superhuman strength to lift the heavy object off the child. Stories like this are not uncommon.

Negative traits are often perceived as bad. However, there is no right or wrong when it comes to traits. We all need both the positive and negative to progress in life. For example, most of the advancements in human rights have come about because the activists were angry enough to protest, exposing the injustice to the world and bringing about the ensuing changes. The Suffragettes' contribution to ensuring women's right to vote in the UK is an apt example of this.

Personality

What constitutes your personality? Your personality is a combination of traits that form your distinctive character. There are numerous personality tests, most of them designed for the office environment. However, these are restrictive because they only focus on the work aspect of your life to the exclusion of the other areas.

We will not be focusing on your personality because, truth be told, you probably know your personality better than anyone. And even if you are unsure you can always ask those nearest and dearest to you. What we will say however is that your personality can change over time, perhaps triggered by significant life events, changes to your environment or simply life experience. For example, some people can be very shy when they are young but become more confident as they grow older.

> Your personality can change over time

When you step into what you were born to do you need to be courageous enough to let who you truly are be seen. The benefits of this are twofold. It allows for personal growth as you begin to access all the traits you need and, in addition, your personality shines because you are no longer hiding behind your insecurities.

The truth about introverts and extroverts

Are you an introvert or an extrovert? There are a lot of misconceptions around these terms. An introvert is normally perceived as someone who is quiet or withdrawn. On the other hand, an extrovert is perceived as someone who is outspoken or lively.

The original meanings behind these terms are slightly different and have been altered over time. The truth is that introverts and extroverts are defined not by how they present to the world but where they draw their energy from. An introvert gets their energy from within. They need to have time to themselves. If they spend a lot of time with other people it is absolutely important that they get their dose of alone time to re-energise. Alone time does not necessarily mean being alone but it does refer to the absence of interaction with others. So someone may have a bubbly outgoing personality but still be an introvert.

An extrovert, on the other hand, gets their energy from interacting with other people. They find it very difficult to cope on their own for extended periods of time. These people tend to have networks or connections that they can call on when required. An extrovert can be a quiet person but is happier being in the company of others.

With respect to what you were born to do, you need to understand what increases your energy and what drains your energy.

For example, if you are an extrovert working in an office alone with little or no interaction with others, your health and well-being can be affected. So whatever it was you were born to do will require having a network of people around you to work with.

Similarly, if you are an introvert constantly having to interact with a large number of people your health and well-being will be affected as well. Whatever it is that you were born to do will require ample time and space away from others to recharge your energy.

Exercise: Are you an introvert, extrovert or just plain shy?

For this exercise you will be using the form in Appendix 6 – 'Are you an Introvert, Extrovert or just plain shy?'. You can download the pdf version of this form at www.findingyourtruthbook.com

Complete the questions answering yes or no and total the number of yeses in each of the three sections. The section with the highest total will indicate whether you are an introvert, extrovert or shy.

We have included a section on 'Shy' for the simple reason that people who are shy are often mistaken for being introverted. Shyness is a trait or personality which can change over time.

However, whether you are an introvert or extrovert does not change.

Complete the exercise in Appendix 6.

Understanding your results

It could be that you get a very clear result in sections 1 and 2, where you have four or more 'Yeses' in one section and four or more 'Nos' in the other. The highest number will indicate if you are an introvert or extrovert.

> If you are an introvert then you will need to find balance in your day to day life so that you get time to yourself to re-energise your batteries. This can be spending time in the garden, having a long bath, meditation or going for a walk or run.

> If you are an extrovert then ensure that you have access to a network of friends or family. Perhaps you can arrange get-togethers or join social groups where people meet frequently.

It could be that you don't get a very clear result in sections 1 and 2 and that you have an equal number of 'Yeses' and 'Nos'. In this case, you can get your energy from either being on your own or being with others. But please note the following:

> This could also indicate that you have never really examined this aspect of yourself. Perhaps you may want to pay closer attention to how you feel with respect to your energy when you are around people or when you are alone, with a view to retaking the test later.

> The more you step into what you were born to do, the truth of who you really are will reveal itself and over time it presents more clearly. If you are stepping onto your path we advise that you re-take the test within a few months.

If could be that you scored four or more on 'Shy'.

Shyness is usually an indication of an insecurity which most likely has its root in fear. It will be worthwhile to understand what is driving this insecurity and gently find ways to work through it as it will hold you back in life. Perhaps attend a course or seek professional advice.

Shyness may also indicate that you are not comfortable with the work you are presently doing. As you progress through this book and start stepping into what you were born to do, you may find that your shyness dissipates over time.

Knowing whether you are an introvert or extrovert is critical for your health and well-being. Having this awareness allows you to properly manage your energy. As you follow your path, you will find that your energy naturally increases over time.

What is your Preferred Representational System?

Your representational system is the way you process information around you. It has its roots in Neural Linguistic Programming (NLP) which is an approach to communication, personal development and psychotherapy. According to NLP, we interact with the world using our five senses of sight (Visual), hearing (Auditory), touch (Kinaesthetic), taste (Gustatory) and smell (Olfactory). Another category called 'Auditory Digital' was created for those who process by internal dialogue.

Everyone uses all the representational systems. However, the one we use the most often is considered our Preferred Representational System. It is the one we use for decision-making and interpreting information. It is also present in our everyday language when we communicate with others.

The work you were born to do is an extension of who you are already. So it is only through understanding the nuances of how you function that you will be able to a) ensure you choose the right path and b) utilise your personal nature so that you are in flow. Most people are not in flow because what they do goes against who they are, causing an energetic friction in their lives. Your Preferred Representational System will help guide you to find the perfect environmental conditions for you in terms of teaching, learning, decision-making and communicating. Because you are perfectly suited to that environment you will be in flow with the potential to thrive.

> The work you were born to do is an extension of who you are already.

EXERCISE: Finding your Preferred Representational System.

For this exercise you will be using the assessment form in Appendix 7 and Appendix 8 to calculate the results. You can download the pdf versions of these forms at www.findingyour truthbook.com

This exercise focuses on the four most commonly used Representational Systems which are Visual, Auditory, Kinaesthetic and Auditory Digital.

Guidelines for finding your Preferred Representational System

1. **As you review the questions take some time to think about past situations, remembering how you felt at the time, to get an accurate reading.** Choose two or more examples to confirm.

   Once you have confirmed in your mind how you felt then record the most appropriate answer using the following rating system:

4 - *Almost always*

3 - *Often*

2 - *Sometimes*

1 - *Almost never*

Every question must utilise all four answers above without repetition. Assign the value that best suits your answer. For example, using question 1, your answers may look like this:

2 - It feels right to me

1 - I hear it and it sounds right to me

4 - I see it and it looks great

3 - I review it and it fits my criteria

2. **Once you have answered all five questions, go to Appendix 8 and follow the instructions to ascertain your Preferred Representational System.**

Understanding your results

The Representational System with the highest total will be your preferred choice. You may have a clear winner. If not, you may have more than one total that is close in value with perhaps no more than a two-point difference. In this case, you have more than one Preferred Representational System to draw on.

What does this mean for you?

Here we will explore how the different representational systems show up in our daily lives.

Visual

If your Preferred Representational System is visual then you tend to prefer processing information visually. Some of your characteristics can include:

- Needing to see something before you can make a decision
- Remembering things better if you have a picture of it in your mind
- Wanting to see the big picture
- Using words such as see, imagine, look. Example: 'This does not look right'.
- Being more easily distracted by visual activity than noise
- Needing to be seen and interested in how things look
- The use of visual material such as flip charts, powerpoint slides, whiteboards, diagrams, handout, colours and props

Kinaesthetic

If your Preferred Representational System is Kinaesthetic you tend to prefer processing information by feeling. Some of your characteristics can include:

- Making decisions based on your gut feelings
- Dressing for comfort rather than appearance
- A slower speech pattern that allows time to process how you are feeling about a topic and preferring others to speak slower for the same reason
- Using words such as feel and touch. Example: 'This does not feel right'.

- Being able to sense the energy of a room and the people within it
- Affectionate behaviour; for example, touching and being touched by friends, family, co-workers, partners in the form of handshakes, hugs, pats on back, etc.
- The use of touching and holding equipment and materials when teaching or learning, often including experiential exercises

Auditory

If your Preferred Representational System is auditory then you tend to prefer processing information by listening. Some of your characteristics can include:

- Talking to yourself
- Being easily distracted by noise
- Preferring to communicate via language than the written word
- Having greater awareness of subtle changes in voice tonality, pitch, speed and volume
- Needing to be heard
- The use of words such as hear, listen or sound. Example: 'This does not sound right'.
- A natural ability to be an excellent listener
- A tendency to ask questions and engage in discussions

Auditory Digital

If your Preferred Representational System is auditory digital then you tend to prefer processing information through internal dialogue much more than the auditory people. Some of your characteristics can include:

- A need to understand and make sense of the world
- Having conversations in your head or imagining conversations with others
- Thinking things through before deciding on a course of action
- A need to have clear steps and procedures
- A preference for logical and practical-based solutions
- A need for a library of information to quell the search for greater understanding

Applying your Preferred Representational System

Knowing your Preferred Representational System gives you get a better understanding of the way you prefer to process information. This then gives an indication of where you will perform the strongest. If you are visual then industries that focus on the visual would work well for you, such as graphic design or creative arts. If you are auditory any industries that focus on listening will work well for you, such as the music industry, conflict resolutions or any therapies involving conversation and listening skills. If you are kinaesthetic touch and intuitive therapies, the textile industry, creative arts with a focus on sculpture or moulding and the like are ideal. If you are auditory digital you will be at home in industries that focus on teaching disciplines, sciences, the financial industry and inventions.

We have only given a few examples but you can do further research now that you are more aware of your Preferred Representational System.

Final Instruction

When you are comfortable with your answers, transfer the following to your results page:

- Whether you are an introvert or extrovert
- Your Preferred Representational System

Final Words

It is perhaps useful to test the results from the exercises in this chapter to see if they reflect the truth of who you are. You may want to do this on a day to day basis. In the case of the introvert and extrovert exercise be aware of your energy levels on your own and in crowds, and test to see if your answers support this. In the case of the representational system notice which format (visual, auditory, etc.) keeps you engaged and which ones make you switch off. And again see if this is in-line with the results you received. If not then redo the exercises at a later date and retest to ensure your results fully support who you are. Sometimes it is only through time and awareness that you are able to answer the questions with conviction.

9 Energetic Qualities

The 9 Energetic Qualities is another aspect of your Inherent Nature™. As this is quite a broad area we have devoted the next chapter to introducing you to this ancient wisdom. Enjoy!

CHAPTER 5

AN INTRODUCTION TO THE 9 ENERGETIC QUALITIES

Background

The 9 Energetic Qualities are based primarily on the ancient I Ching influence and, in particular, two books: *The Yellow Emperor's Classic (of Internal Medicine)* and *The Green Satchel Classic (Internal Medicine and Feng Shui)*. These books contain knowledge and philosophy from the Far-East dating back approximately 5,000 years.

Originally used in China and later refined in Japan, it was born out of long-term research conducted by the Emperor's scribes over 2,500 years. The scribes observed and documented the personalities of people who came to the Emperor's courts. They looked at how their personalities correlated back to patterns within nature with reference to their date of birth.

As such, the 9 Energetic Qualities are a very ancient form of numerology. Because these observations were conducted over such a long period of time and with a very large population, the qualities of the 9 Energetic Qualities are now highly refined and accurate.

> The 9 Energetic Qualities are a very ancient form of numerology.

Knowledge of the 9 Energetic Qualities provides a guide to understanding your personality, honing in on your specific character and behaviours. In this book we are introducing you to the concept of the 9 Energetic Qualities, only in so far as they relate to discovering the real you and the work you were born to do. It outlines the key areas we cover on our *Discover the Work You Were Born to Do* live and online courses.

Exercise: Calculating your 9 Energetic Qualities numbers

As the 9 Energetic Qualities are based on numerology, your date of birth is used to calculate three specific numbers. These numbers will help you to understand the subtleties of your underlying nature, which may not be apparent at first. However, once you understand these qualities, you will realise how much it influences your everyday actions, choices and decisions. For the exercise you will be using the tables in Appendix 9, the Energetic Qualities Calculations. You can download the pdf version of these tables at www.findingyourtruthbook.com

> These numbers will help you to understand the subtleties of your underlying nature

Guidelines to calculating your 9 Energetic Qualities numbers

1. **Calculate your first number by using your year of birth.**

    In Appendix 9, Step 1, locate your year of birth on the Complete Year Chart table. Look to the top of that column and there are two numbers between one and nine. Use the number in the first row (F) if you are female. Use the number in the second row (M) if you are male. Let's use the date of birth for a female born on 22 June, 1971 to illustrate. Locate 1971 (year of birth) on the table. Look at the top of that column and you will see the number 4 in the row assigned to females. So the first number will be 4.

Special circumstances for those born <u>BEFORE</u> 4/5 February.

*For the purposes of the 9 Energetic Qualities, the year starts from 4/5 February (based on the solar calendar) and not on 1 January as in the traditional western calendar. So if you were born anytime between 1 January and 3 February inclusive, you would use the previous year to calculate your first number. For example, if you were male and born 26 January, 1963 you would locate **1962** and look to the top of that column at 'M' for male, which is the number 2.*

Special circumstances applying to those born <u>ON</u> 4/5 February.

In traditional Chinese culture the start of spring occurs on the 4/5 February. These dates straddle the end of one year and the beginning of another. However, it is based on the solar calendar rather than the traditional western calendar, so these dates are not set in stone. This is similar to the 'cusp' you get when reading horoscopes in astrology.

These particular dates may relate to either the current year or the previous year. You will need to intuitively sense which qualities of the first number fit you best. For example, if you were born on 5 February, 1975 you will need to check the numbers for both 1974 and 1975 to see which one feels right for you. We suggest you begin by using your actual year of birth first and go through the full process of calculating your three numbers. If this does not feel right to you then repeat the process using the year before.

2. **Calculate your second number by using your month of birth.**

There are three tables in Step 2 (Appendix 9). Each table is labelled with three of the possible nine numbers. Each table has three rows. The top row indicates the month of birth (F for February, M for March, etc.). The second row is labelled 'M' for male with numbers assigned to each month of the year and the third row is labelled 'F' for female with numbers assigned to each month of the year. To get your second number use the table that has your first number in the table heading. Ignore the other two tables. Using the table you have identified look in the first row for your month of birth. Looking down at that column use the number in the second row if you are male or the number in the third row if you are female.

Continuing with our previous example of a female born on 22 June, 1971, as her first number is four you will use the first of the three tables as it contains four in the table heading. As she was born in June you would look across the first row to find June and then look down the June column to the third row as she is female. The number 2, which is indicated here, will be her second number.

3. **Calculate your third number.**

To calculate your third number you will need your first and second numbers in the order they appear and apply them to the table in Step 3. The top row of the table refers to your 'year number' or your first number. The first column refers to your 'month number' or your second number. Locate your first number from the top row and scroll down that column until it intersects with your second number (listed in the first column). This box contains your three relevant numbers.

Continuing with the earlier example of a female born on 22 June, 1971, her first number is four and her second number is two. So in Step 3 look across the top row until you reach the number 4. Then look down that column until you reach the number 2 in the first column. This box contains the numbers 4-2-7, which are her three relevant numbers.

Understanding the roles your numbers play

Although each number has its own unique representation, it is important to note that you possess all the qualities of all three numbers.

Like most things in nature, these qualities can exist in a balanced state or unbalanced state. In a balanced state the qualities are allowed to express themselves in a healthy quantity. An unbalanced state exists when these qualities are expressed in copious amounts leading to obsessive and exhaustive states.

Your first number

The first number is your major influence and the most important of the three numbers. It is seen in Chinese philosophy as the beginning point from which a person expands. It shows you who you are at your deepest core or spiritual self. If allowed full expression it means you are being authentic in the real sense of the word. Stresses and ill health tend to occur when these qualities are restricted in some form.

Your second number

You possess all the attributes and qualities of the second number. In addition, the second number has an influence on the first number by either heightening or dampening it. This number also gives you an understanding of the feelings and behaviours you revert to under stress or when you are upset. However, as this is only an introduction into the 9 Energetic Qualities, this aspect of the second number is more appropriately addressed in our *Building Your Emotional Resilience* training.

Your third number

You possess all the attributes and qualities of the third number. In addition, the third number has an influence on the first and second numbers by either heightening or dampening it. This number shows how you appear to the world and your approach to everyday tasks. When you meet someone it is the influence of this third number that will be visible and this becomes their impression of you.

Understanding what the numbers represent

Before we go into what each of the 9 numbers represents, here is an overall picture to help guide you. Each of the 9 numbers will relate to both a) an aspect of nature and b) a metaphorical place in the family. Together they give you an insight into your Inherent Nature™.

a.   Aspects of nature

Each of the 9 aspects of nature has its own unique qualities. By understanding these qualities you begin to understand your true essence. This is best approached by visualising the aspect of nature, what qualities it would have and then understanding how those qualities shape your personality.

b.   Metaphorical place in the family

Each number, for the most part, is assigned a metaphorical place in the family. You will possess the qualities of this 'metaphorical' person depending on your assigned number. Please note, this is not your actual place in the family but only an assigned one. For example, the number 6 represents the father figure. It may be that you are actually female and the last child in the family but you will display the qualities of a father-like figure.

Understanding the qualities of the numbers is an intuitive process rather than a clear-cut scientific approach. It requires that with each element you ponder the characteristics and how they are reflected in you.

Exploring each of the 9 Energetic Qualities

Please note that we are presenting the qualities here only in their balanced state.

Energetic quality #1

Element: **Sea water**

Place in the family: **Middle son**

The nature of sea water is that it can be calm and gentle on the surface but with strong moving currents underneath. It is deep, powerful and expansive.

Key qualities:

- Your key-word is **truth**. You are relentless in your search for the truth.

- As with all water energies, you are highly creative, in touch with your emotions and there is a flow to your energy

- You are very adaptable

- Like an iceberg, you allow others to only see a small bit of you, keeping most of what you are thinking under the surface

- Privacy and quiet time are important to you
- As the metaphorical teenage boy you are very adventurous and outgoing

Energetic quality #2

Element: **Earth**

Place in the family: **Mother**

The image that is conjured here is that of mother earth: nurturing, nourishing and healing. It is a slow moving, deliberate and grounding energy.

Key qualities:

- Your key-word is **nurturing** and your focus is always on how you can help others
- Like the metaphorical mother, you have unlimited patience and perseverance
- You are kind, thoughtful and supportive when dealing with others
- You have a mother's intuition and you are a natural healer
- As a natural supporter, you can adapt yourself to any role required
- You approach things practically and pragmatically

Energetic quality #3

Element: **Thunder**

Place in the family: **Eldest son**

The image that is conjured here is an explosive force of energy: clearing the air, preceded by the illumination of lightning.

Key qualities:

- Your key-word is **inspiration** which comes in flashes like the proverbial light bulb moments

- Thunder energy tend to be initiators, ground-breakers or visionaries

- Fast and vibrant, you are more concerned with doing rather than being and will not hang around before moving on to the next thing

- You are a true optimist, confident you can handle whatever comes your way

- The thunder energy pushes outwards so it is difficult for you to see your many wonderful qualities

- As the metaphorical eldest son you are a natural leader who likes to be in control

Energetic quality #4

Element: **Wind**

Place in the family: **Eldest daughter**

You feel the effects of wind although you do not see it. It has no boundaries nor edges. It blows everywhere.

Key qualities:

- Your key-word is **revealing**. As the wind is everywhere it is able to uncover any hidden motives and bring clarity to situations.

- As the wind cannot be contained freedom and space are vital to you

- The ability of wind to change direction means that you are very flexible with an easy going nature

- Changes are usually made at the drop of a hat, and usually done instinctively and intuitively

- The unseen nature of wind gives an air of mystery about you

- As the metaphorical eldest daughter you are second in command after mother and can step up when required

Energetic quality #5

Element: **Vortex**

Place in the family: **Has aspects of each member of the family**

The vortex energy is a whirling mass containing aspects of the energy of all the other numbers but grounded by the earth energy. If you are a female you will display some of the qualities of the earth energy (#2). If you are male you will display some of the energies of the mountain energy (#8).

- Key aspect is '**Jack of all trades**'. You tend to be an all-rounder, having versatility and wide-ranging skills.

- As you have an innate earth energy you are always drawn to helping others

- The vortex energy is like a gravitational pull so people naturally gravitate towards you and you are happiest when you are central to something

- As you are an all-rounder you strive to be self-sufficient, rarely seeking help from others

- With this whirling quality you generate a lot of energy and so can keep going for a long time

- You can take on the metaphorical role of any place in the family when required

Energetic quality #6

Element: **Heaven**

Place in the family: **Father**

The heaven energy is overseeing, magnanimous and expansive, with an upward moving quality.

- Key-word is **respect**. The overseeing role of heaven commands respect to yourself and others, and must be given and earned.

- There is a natural upward movement of energy towards the heavens, so you will want to move ahead in whatever position you hold

- Having a bird's eye view from above, you have the ability to see both the big picture and the fine details

- This also allows you to see potential problems and pre-empt them

- Your energy is deliberate and careful in your actions and choices. You will happily ignore anything that does not serve you.

- In the metaphorical father role you are a natural leader and provider, ensuring the well-being of anyone in your charge

Energetic quality #7

Element: **Lake**

Place in the family: **Youngest daughter**

The lake energy is very calm on the surface with great depth beneath.

- Key-word is **tranquillity**. There is a very calming nature to this energy.

- You have the ultimate poker-face as no one can

guess from your expression what you are thinking or feeling

- The beauty of the lake allows a creative quality, bringing grace and elegance to everything you touch

- Your environment is important to you. It needs to be pleasing, clean and tidy.

- As the waters of the lake run deep so does you quest for clarity and you are naturally inquisitive

- Being the metaphorical youngest daughter there is a pure and innocent quality in your approach to life

Energetic quality #8

Element: **Mountain**

Place in the family: **Youngest son**

The mountain energy reaches upwards and has an overlooking quality. It is also the masculine earth energy and, as with all earth energies, there is a natural caring aspect.

- Key-word is **strength.** Mountain energy gives you stability and resilience, allowing you to easily bounce back from any challenge.

- As it is impossible to hide a mountain you want to be seen and take charge

- The structural form of the mountain masks the softness of the earth energy which means that you can appear strong on the outside, but there is a softness to your inner nature

- Within a mountain you will find a cave, which means occasionally you need to retreat inwards to recharge and regain your strength and gain new insights

- As this is an earth-related energy you are very grounded and like practical, tangible solutions

- As the metaphorical youngest son there is a love of adventure, exploring and pioneering

Energetic quality #9

Element: **Fire**

Place in the family: **Middle daughter**

The fire energy is a bringer of light and illumination, transforming that which it touches.

- Key-word is **transformation**. Everything that fire touches is changed into something new and different.
- The fire energy brings light in an outward direction. Your intelligence allows you to reveal all, leaving nothing in shadow.
- The warmth of the fire means that you are incredibly warm, open-hearted and affectionate
- Fire constantly needs to be fuelled, as do you. Change and variety are very important to you.
- When put into the spotlight you naturally shine
- As the metaphorical middle daughter you may have a rebellious nature and can challenge the status quo

Final instruction

Record your 9 Energetic Quality Numbers and any key-words relating to them on your 'Results Page'.

Final Words

As stated before, this is only an introduction into the 9 Energetic Qualities and we have briefly touched the surface of this very powerful tool. To go as in-depth as we would like to would require us to write a whole other book! However, you can have access to a deeper profile through a session with David Nassim. David is our guide in this field and has devoted the last fifteen years of his life to researching and mastering the 9 Energetic Qualities. David can be contacted at <u>david.nassim@yahoo.co.uk</u>

CHAPTER 6

UNCOVERING YOUR TALENTS

In the last two chapters we looked at your Inherent Nature™. In this chapter we will be looking at your many talents, both discovered and undiscovered. Whatever it is you were born to do, you must have a talent for it. However, sometimes we only find out that we have a talent for something when we approach something new for the first time. Up until then we probably did not know that this talent existed.

> Sometimes we only find out that we have a talent for something when we approach something new for the first time.

But expressing your talent does not equate to happiness. For you to be happy the use of your talents must be supported by your Inherent Nature™. For example, looking at footage of Susan Boyle, the extraordinarily talented singer, it appears that she is very uncomfortable in the limelight, leading us to believe that she is private and perhaps introverted. So in order for her to be happy using her talent she would be better suited to recording studios and private audiences away from

> Expressing your talent does not equate to happiness.

the limelight. If continually pressured to be in the limelight she would be very stressed and uncomfortable. This can also be seen in Hollywood where a myriad of very talented actors and entertainers resort to drugs and alcohol to cope. It could be that they are not allowed to be themselves but have to project a certain Hollywood persona which directly conflicts with the core of who they are. On the other hand, Richard Branson has a talent for business, spotting opportunities and acting on them. His unique talent is strongly supported by his Inherent Nature™, which clearly shines through in the work he does in the form of his adventurous, fun loving and energetic personality.

Guidelines to uncovering your talents

1. **Have an open mind and let your answers flow.**

   Approach each question objectively and intuitively to get the most out of this exercise. We all have many talents. It could be that because we have not used them for a while we may have forgotten that they exist.

2. **Think sequentially and cover all aspects of your life.**

   We have a tendency to focus on what is currently going on in our lives and forget the past, which may hold vital clues to your talents. Appendix 2 – 'Key Areas and Transitions in Your Life' comes in very handy here, helping you to cover all aspects of your life both horizontally (the eight primary areas) and *vertically* (the chronological sequence of your life).

3. **Include everything you can think of.**

   Don't dismiss anything regardless of how bizarre it might appear to you or others. You are unique and, as such, you will have unique talents.

4. **Answer all the questions to the best of your ability.**

   The quality of the outcome of this exercise is directly proportional to the quality of your input. This means the more engaged and committed you are, the better the results. Superficial engagement equals superficial results. Give 100%.

5. **Write as many talents as you can.**

   Don't limit yourself because you think you are writing too much. In fact, it is better to write too much rather than too little. These answers will eventually be shortlisted based on your Inherent Nature™ so write as many talents as you can think of. But remember point 2, try to avoid duplications.

The exercise is based on a series of questions. These questions are designed to help you to dig deeper, think broader and draw out the relevant information. You may not have answers
to all the questions but try to answer as many of them as possible. Use a notepad to record your answers.

Exercise: What are your talents?

As stated above, you need to understand what your skills and talents are in order to have the path of least resistance to the work you were born to do.

Step 1

Begin by asking your friends, family and co-workers what your talents are.

We sometimes fail to recognise our own talents or perhaps take for granted the things that we do easily and effortlessly. For example, one of our clients, Sonia, believed she was very bossy with her sisters, always taking control of the situation. Her sisters, however, looked at this as being very organised rather than bossy or controlling, much to Sonia's surprise.

So ask as many people as possible what they think your talents are and record it in your notepad.

Step 2

Answer the following questions to help you uncover your existing talents:

1. **What do people tell you about you that you tend not to believe?**

   We tend to be very dismissive when we are told we are good at something. However, it is easier for someone else to see in you what you cannot see in yourself. Using Appendix 2, look back over your life to jog your memory for comments or conversations where people complimented or showed an appreciation for something you were directly involved in.

2. **What are you naturally good at?**

   As mentioned above, we have a tendency to take for granted the things we do easily, not realising that this task may not be as easy for others to do. For example, Nikki was responsible for organising meetings at her previous employment. She was always praised by the board members for doing an exemplary job and making sure that the events flowed smoothly. However, she just thought to herself, 'What's the big deal? Anybody can do this', because it came to her so easily and naturally. But in reality we know it takes a very special skill set to be able to organise meetings well. We often fail to recognise the things we do without blinking an eyelid as talents.

In order to help you uncover the things that you are naturally good at, start by breaking it down as follows:

- Recall a process or situation that you were involved in. It could be a routine undertaking or just a one-off. Example: planning a birthday party or simply preparing a meal.

- Break down the process into tasks

- Note all the tasks that came very easily to you and record them in your notepad

- Repeat for a few different situations

3. **In your current occupation, what do you do outside of your job description?**

Our talents naturally come out wherever we are and they are difficult to suppress. You will often see this showing up in your job where you are not specifically told to do it but you do it anyway. For example, in her career as an accountant, Michele was constantly teaching and training other members of staff, although this was not part of her job description. She is now following the work she was born to do which involves teaching and training to a large degree.

To help you answer this question, sequentially review past jobs you have had. Consider all the things you did that was not in your job specification and record them in your notepad.

4. **What do people automatically turn to you for?**

People will turn to you for help with things that you are good at. For example, we turn to our colleague, Simone, for help with our power-point presentations. She has an extraordinary talent for creating visually effective slides. So what do people automatically turn to you for? Record your answers in your notepad.

5. **What do you enjoy doing that others may consider a chore?**

We tend to enjoy certain tasks simply because they come very easily to us. This indicates a talent or skill for it. On the other hand, someone else may look at the same task and consider it a chore simply because they don't have a natural talent for it and it is much harder for them to do. For example, Tammy thinks that doing research is very easy and will jump at the task, whereas Carol thinks it is the worst thing in the world to do. So list the things on your notepad that you not only enjoy but you are also good at.

6. **What do you really do well that no one taught you to do?**

Although skills are important and once learnt and mastered they become a talent, there are things we do really well that we were never taught. In this question, these are the talents we are looking for. For example, Michael has been curious about how things work all his life, constantly pulling apart and putting back together gadgets and household appliances. He is now a sought-after mechanical engineer without ever having any formal training.

Using Appendix 2, think over your life for the things that you may have learnt on your own and record them in your notepad.

7. **Was there anything you enjoyed doing that you were discouraged from developing?**

Our parents, teachers and those in authority often guide us to what they believe is in our best interest.

Sadly, through this, we are sometimes discouraged from developing the things we are drawn to or have a natural talent for, simply because they may not be in line with the family business, not a big earner or not prestigious enough. For example, we heard of a lady who was encouraged by her parents to become a doctor against her will. Her passion was always drawing comic graphics which she was discouraged from doing at a young age. She has now left the medical profession and is actively and happily pursuing a new career in comic graphic design.

You may or may not have been discouraged from developing talents, but if there are any please record those on your notepad as well.

Shortlisting your main talents

You should now have a comprehensive list of what you believe your talents to be. No talent is ever wasted and you can draw on them whenever the situation requires it. Also, bear in mind that new talents will continue to emerge as you explore new areas. To shortlist your main talents, do the following steps:

> No talent is ever wasted and you can draw on them whenever the situation requires it.

1. Go through your answers and highlight any recurring or common themes.

2. Have to hand your shortlist of activities you are drawn to, which you determined from Chapter 3 (remember these activities already map to your Inner Codes™)

3. Now review your list of talents against this shortlist of activities

4. Highlight as many of those talents that can directly be utilised in the expression of your shortlisted activities

5. Also, highlight any talents that map back to your 9 Energetic Qualities (Chapter 5)

Final Instruction

Transfer all the talents that you have highlighted to your 'Results Page'.

Final Words

At this stage you are two-thirds of the way to getting all the pertinent information to help you understand the truth of who you are and the work you were born to do. Every aspect involves a) understanding the core of who you are and then b) aligning your talents and passions with that core. This allows you to be who you were meant to be whilst pursuing a job, career or business that you were naturally designed for.

CHAPTER 7

HEROES, FRUSTRATIONS AND VISIONS

This chapter is slightly different in its approach. We are going off the beaten track to gain a deeper understanding of what drives us, what frustrates us and what we aspire to, in order to understand a little more about our truth.

The previous chapters, particularly Chapters 3 and 6, dealt with the activities you are drawn to and your talents. These are the two most common methods used when trying to understand what you were born to do. However, in this chapter you are going to use additional methods both to confirm or reinforce your previous results and to gain new insights. The approach here will be to look at three seemingly unrelated areas: 1) your heroes, 2) your frustrations and 3) your visions, all of which, if answered correctly, will lead you to the right path.

Your heroes

Your heroes in this particular context are the people you look up to or admire. As we go through life we gravitate towards certain people. These people may be in the public eye, closer to home or characters in a book, play or film. We are drawn to these people because there is something about them that resonates with us. Most times we never really explore why this is so. The next exercise is about understanding why you have chosen these particular people to be your heroes.

Exercise: Who are your heroes?

Step 1

Choose three people who you admire or look up to.

We are looking for the people who really inspire you. You may be drawn to reading their biography or any other information about them. Maybe you are inspired by their moral code, the work they do or the cause they represent. There is no right or wrong. Whatever the reason for your choices, they will be valid. Now choose your top three. They can be:

- Living or dead
- Fictional or real
- Family or friends

Again, be truthful with your choices regardless of what others may think. Remember, these exercises are about you and for you and no one will have privy to your answers unless you wish to share them. So if one of the people you admire is Bart Simpson no one here is going to judge you.

Step 2

For the three people that you chose in Step 1, what are their traits and what is it about them that you admire?

Write as much as you can in your notepad.

Step 3

Choose the top three traits from your list and transfer them to your 'Results Page'.

The relevance of this exercise

Like our activities in Chapter 3, we are drawn to our heroes for a reason. In Chapter 4 we talked about traits and personalities and the fact that we have all the traits within us. So it follows that we also have all the traits of our heroes

> We also have all the traits of our heroes within us.

within us. It may be that you are already living these traits. If so, great, you are on the right path. On the other hand, it could be that they need to be activated and nurtured. You aspire to express these traits but there is perhaps within you a limiting belief that you can't be as good as that person or you can't be that way. In this case, you need to identify what the limiting belief is and work through it.

The activities you are drawn to (Chapter 3) and your talents (Chapter 6) are stepping stones for you to eventually become your own version of your heroes. Your heroes become the ideal and you use them as a guide on your path. As you evolve and gain greater clarity your heroes may change. This is normal.

Word of caution

Heroes are not to be worshipped. They are there to be emulated, to guide the way for you. Too often you give away your power to the gurus or the experts believing them to be somehow better than you are. It is impossible to compare yourself with anyone else. You are on your own unique journey just as they are. The most you can do is be true to your own path and let your heroes be your guides.

> Heroes are not to be worshipped. They are there to be emulated, to guide the way for you.

Your frustrations

Anger and frustration are often thought of as negative emotions. But like everything else in the world, there is a reason for them. Some of the most profound advancements in humanity were made by individuals who were angry and frustrated about an injustice. They were frustrated enough to put themselves on the line for what they believed in. One example is Rosa Parks, an African-American civil rights activist. In 1955, she refused to give up her seat in the coloured section to a white passenger after the white section was filled. This led to the lifting of the law requiring segregation on public buses and contributed to fighting for equal rights for all in America. Another well-known example is Mahatma Gandhi. He was an Indian nationalist leader who was frustrated with the poverty and lack of fair treatment in his homeland. This eventually led to India gaining independence from the British. As a result, he has and is still inspiring movements for civil rights and freedom across the world.

> Some of the most profound advancements in humanity were made by individuals who were angry and frustrated about an injustice.

In the following exercise we are going to examine your frustrated side to see who or what is pushing your buttons.

Exercise: Follow your frustrations

Step 1

Think about your three top frustrations.

- This may be in relation to people you know well or randomly met in passing
- The incident will usually stay on your mind for a long period after it has happened

- Even after years have passed you can still recall the incident in detail

Please note that these people may not have done anything to you. They may have just made an innocent statement in passing. However, this statement will leave you really frustrated and make you want to shake some sense into them.

You may not identify your top frustrations immediately, so take some time to think about it. When you recall the incident, tap into your emotions to get really specific on what was frustrating you.

Step 2

For each of your top three frustrations answer the following questions:

- What did they say or do that pushed your buttons?
- What do you want to change about them?
- What were you thinking as you were listening to or looking at them?
- What do you want to shout to them about?
- What are they not doing that you feel they should be doing?

Record your answers in your notepad.

Step 3

Record your answer to Step 3 on your 'Results Page'.

You may not be able to see the link as yet but your top frustration will play a critical role in the work you were born to do.

Your visions

There are two types of visions. The first, which we will refer to as conscious visions, are those that you create in your mind on purpose, otherwise known as your imagination. The second, which we will refer to as random visions, appear like a flash in your mind or in dreams without you having control over what happens. We will explore both types in this section.

It is worthwhile noting that everything that has been created in this world was first created in the mind. The books and other materials on manifesting your dreams are all very clear in that you have to be able to see it before you can achieve it. All high achievers in this world have an absolutely clear vision of what they want. The projections of our mind, whether conscious or random, give clues to our aspirations. Our talents and the activities we are drawn to are based in the past and present, whereas our visions are projections of the future. These visions also need to be aligned with the results of all the exercises you have done up to this point.

> The projections of our mind, whether conscious or random, give clues to our aspirations.

Let us now look at each type of vision in further detail.

Exercise: Conscious visions

In this exercise we will be asking you to project your thoughts into the future, which gives you an indication of your aspirations. Some of you may not be used to thinking in this way, however, it is worthwhile persevering. This exercise uses the concept of future pacing, which means that you start in the future and then create a path back to your present reality. Use your notepad to record the answers to the following questions:

1. **What does your idea of a perfect world look like?**

    If you can imagine a perfect world, what would it look like? What would it feel like? What would it sound like? This projection is at a very high, abstract level. For example, the vast majority of the population (especially in the Miss World and Miss Universe pageants, not forgetting the film, *Miss Congeniality*) all want world peace! This may also be your idea of a perfect world, however, everyone's idea of what world peace looks like is very different. It may be that world peace is not your idea of the perfect world. World peace or not, use your notepad to write down what your idea of a perfect world is. You may write as much or as little as you wish.

2. **What would your perfect world look like on a practical level?**

   In question 1 you gave a very high, abstract vision of your perfect world. In this question, we would like you to bring it down to earth. What we mean here is, what are the people practically doing in order to create this perfect world?

3. **If you were to teach the tasks needed to create this perfect world, what would these tasks be?**

   In other words, what do you have to teach the people in order for them to be able to help you create this perfect world?

4. **What role did you specifically play in shaping this perfect world?**

   Of all the tasks that you are able to teach or do to help you create this perfect world, which task was it that you chose to do?

5. **Which one or more of the Inner Codes™ is this role supporting?**

   More than likely, the role that you are playing is an extension of one or more of your top 5 Inner Codes™.

Your Inner Codes™ are such a core part of who you are that when you project into the future you cannot help but project your Inner Codes™ as well. This exercise helps to reveal a practical task that will be in perfect alignment with your Inner Codes™.

6. Record your answer to question 4 on your 'Results Page'.

Never underestimate the power of having a vision that exceeds where you are now. In fact, this becomes your guiding light and focal point to actually get you there.

Exercise: Random visions

According to Sigmund Freud, renowned psychologist, the mind can be divided into three different levels:

- Your conscious mind which filters all information
- The preconscious mind which is your ordinary memory
- Your unconscious mind which stores all remaining information

We will now give you a simplified version of how these three levels operate.

Research has shown that our mind absorbs anywhere from 2 to 40 million bits at a time (research is highly variable in this area but they all agree that it is millions). However, if your brain had to process this amount of information it would overload. In order to prevent this, the information is filtered through our values and belief systems. So our conscious mind only absorbs 7 (+/-2) bits of information at a time and is only aware of this limited amount of information.

The preconscious mind is where your ordinary memory is stored. That is, all the 7 (+/-2) bits of information you have accumulated over the years is stored here. We may not be conscious at all times of what is stored in the preconscious mind, but we do have the ability to access it at any point in time by simply remembering.

Everything else will be stored in your unconscious mind. This constitutes everything that is outside of your conscious awareness. Your dreams, intuition and random visions are a product of your unconscious mind. These can appear to be very weird or have no timeline, simply because there are no filters or belief systems in your unconscious mind.

Step 1

Note down any random dreams, intuitions or visions that you may have dismissed in the past.

Please note, you may or may not remember these. We all have dreams and visions; however, we sometimes tend to dismiss them. So have a careful think and then use your notepad to record the answers.

Step 2

Record your answer to Step 1 on your 'Results Page'.

If you cannot remember them at this point you may want to make a note to pay attention in the future. To help you along, it is worthwhile to take time out to be quiet every day, whether to meditate or just to be mindful. This will help you to reduce the chatter of your conscious mind and allow the intuition and visions of your unconscious mind to surface.

Step 3

Common themes.

There should be a common theme running through your answers to all of the exercises in this chapter. If there is then you are on the right track. If there isn't you may want to take some time to really think about these questions and redo them at a later stage.

CHAPTER 8

UNCOVERING YOUR GENIUS

Yes, you do have a genius

Most people have an air of disbelief whenever they are told that they have a genius. They seem to think anything 'genius' related must be linked to a high IQ or extraordinary artistic talent. The truth is everyone has a genius. Like your Inner Codes™, it has been with you since birth and is evident in all areas of your life. But your genius will really shine through and be more noticeable in the activities you are drawn to do.

> The truth is everyone has a genius.

Our genius, like our Inherent Nature™ and Inner Codes™, is an integral part of who we are. The working of our genius is an Internal Process™ that happens unconsciously and automatically. Most times we do not even realise it exists. If you are aware of it you don't recognise it as your genius or anything special. And because it comes to you so naturally you think everybody else can do it.

Uncovering Your Genius

Uncovering our genius is about noticing what you do when you are not noticing what you do. It sounds like a tongue twister but it pretty much does what it says on the tin. It is about bringing to light that action that happens so automatically and instantaneously for you.

> Uncovering our genius is about noticing what you do when you are not noticing what you do.

For the purpose of this exercise we will be occasionally referring to two of our clients, Gabrielle and David, and the process by which they revealed their genius.

Attributes of your genius

Here are some descriptions of what your genius constitutes. This is to give you a starting point to help you to uncover your genius.

a. **It is an 'action' process.**

   Whatever your genius is, it takes the form of an action. It will always relate to how you perform a particular task whether it is related to your work, home or social life. For example, Gabrielle's genius is 'creating flow'. David's genius is 'finding the truth'.

b. **It is a common thread that runs through everything you do.**

   What you do at home may be completely different from what you do at work, but your initial thought process will be the same in both situations, although this may not yet be apparent to you. It is this approach that begins to give an indication of your genius and forms a common thread that runs through everything you do.

In the case of Gabrielle's 'creating flow', flow is created in every task at work, in the home and even in arranging social engagements. Her home and everything in it is always organised. There are systems and processes set up at work to ensure everything runs smoothly and is flowing. Anything that poses an obstacle to the smooth flow is pre-empted and dealt with promptly.

David's 'finding the truth' is easy to see in his work as a healer because he can quickly get to the truth of the client's problem. In his home life materiality is often disregarded and viewed as unimportant to him because, in his teachings of spirituality, the material world is not regarded as truth. In social engagements he gravitates towards authenticity as these individuals are being true to themselves. He finds it a challenge to deal with anyone who is inauthentic. The magic about David's ability to find the truth is that he can tell the difference between who is authentic and who isn't in the blink of an eye because that's his genius. For the rest of us this is not an automatic process and people around us can, and do, deceive us.

We have chosen these two very different examples to show you that, regardless of what your genius is, it will permeate your life and it will influence your lifestyle, choices and habits.

c. **It is usually uncovered first in the form of a question.**

Your genius is a solution to a particular question you ask yourself. What happens is that your mind automatically finds the solution without you even being aware that you asked yourself a question. Unlocking the question helps to unlock your genius. In the case of Gabrielle and David above, they both had to first unlock their question before they understood their genius. For Gabrielle, her question was, 'How do I make this more effective and efficient?' For David, his question was, 'What is the truth of this situation?'

d. **It is evident in the choices or decisions we make in life.**

Once you understand what your genius is it becomes evident as to how your decisions and choices are made and why you do things the way you do. If Gabrielle needs to make a decision between two options her automatic question will be, 'Which of these two is the most effective and efficient?' She is usually unaware that she is asking this question. If David had the same choice he would choose only that option that he perceives as truth and will ignore the other. If he feels that neither option is the truth he will ignore both.

e. **It is an organic process.**

Don't expect to get this all in one go. It is very much a continual process of uncovering information. Once you start you will probably quickly have an idea circling in your head as to what your genius is. However, this idea will need to be tested and refined, and this process repeated until it proves to be true for all situations (home, work, social life, etc.). It took Gabrielle and David several weeks of introspection and coaching for them to really nail what their genius was.

f. **It elevates your confidence.**

Once you are aware of what your genius is you begin to slowly realise that it is who you are. It is a natural part of you. You do it extraordinarily well and so effortlessly that you begin to understand that you can't be anything else but this. When you accept your genius as truth your confidence grows because you stop second-guessing and doubting yourself. Since uncovering their genius, Gabrielle and David understand exactly where they would thrive and seek out work requiring these skills. Because their genius is intuitive to them they are now highly successful and sought-after. Success breeds confidence, and they both now embrace and own their genius.

Guidelines to uncovering your genius

1. **This is an exercise in self-awareness.**

   As stated above, your genius is not going to be immediately apparent. You have to:

   Choose a few tasks, events or situations in your life

   Go back to your thoughts at the time

   Slow down and dissect your automatic process

   The exercise following these guidelines will offer a few tasks or situations for you to start working with. Please feel free to expand on this with examples of your own choosing.

2. **It is about getting to the common denominator of why you do what you do and why you make the choices you make in your job and everyday life.**

   Once your genius is identified, you will be able to see it working in all aspects of your life as Gabrielle and David did.

3. **To uncover your genius, you need to be aware of your thoughts and, more importantly, your internal dialogue or self-talk.**

   As your genius is very much an automated process, slowing down your thoughts and internal dialogue will bring to light that very important question you ask yourself before your genius springs into action.

4. **You need to name your genius.**

   This is very important because it helps to bring it from the realm of the invisible to the visible. It also makes it easier to understand, explain and use. Following the example above, Gabrielle's genius is 'creating flow'. She is now able to communicate this precisely with others and everyone understands clearly what she does. Same for David. His genius is 'finding the truth' and he is able to communicate this effectively with others.

5. **Keep questioning your answers until you have identified the right words and phrasing of what you believe to be your genius.**

   When Gabrielle was going through her discovery process she first came up with the word 'orderly' but felt it was more than just orderly. She kept drilling down until she realised it was not just about being orderly; the order had to be both effective and efficient. But this was only after several bouts of trial and error before she understood clearly what it was. In the case of David it was perhaps a little more obscure. He hovered around words such as detective, research and intuition until he realised all of these words were aspects of 'finding the truth'. Like Gabrielle, it was a case of trial and error until the right words revealed themselves.

Exercise: Uncovering your genius

We will now take you through a few scenarios to begin the process of uncovering your genius. Remember, you need to go back to specific situations and slow down your thought process.

Step 1

Scenario: You walk into a room for the first time

Think back to a time when you entered a room for the first time. Use a situation that was real; for example, you were visiting somewhere you had never been before. Try, as far as possible, to remember what you were thinking about the room as you were entering. Then answer the following questions if relevant and record the answers in your notepad:

a. What did you think about as you entered the room? Or what bothered you about that room? Or what impressed you about that room?

b. Why did you feel that way?

c. Then ask yourself 'Why?', again in response to your previous answer

d. Repeat the 'Why' process until you can't go any further

e. Highlight any descriptive words that are similar in nature

Step 2

Scenario: Easy and effortlessly.

Think about a minimum of three times in your life when something came to you easily, or when you did something for which you were really pleased with the outcome. You just knew what to do. Then, where possible, answer the following questions and record the answers in your notepad:

a.   What in those situations came naturally to you?

b.   What is the process behind that?

c.   Why is that process so important to you?

d.   Highlight any descriptive words that are similar in nature

Step 3

Scenario: Don't you dare say that!

What would be the one thing that, if people accused you of or labelled you with, you would refute emphatically (even if it is only in your head)? You would probably think to yourself, 'How can they say this about me?' or 'I am so not like that!' It would really offend you. Find a second and third thing. Then, where possible, answer the following questions and record the answers in your notepad:

a.   Why would that bother you?

b.   Write down all the words that come to mind.

c.   Highlight any descriptive words that are similar in nature.

Step 4

Other areas to look at.

As mentioned before, you can choose other situations or scenarios that you can test using the questions in Steps 1 to 3 as guidelines. The objective here is to understand the thought process behind your actions. Below are some other ideas you can explore. Please note that this is surface level only and you will need to drill down further by continually asking yourself 'Why?'. Do this until the words feel as if they are the right fit. Choose three scenarios for questions a, b and c. This will enable you to have a more comprehensive list of words to describe your genius. Record the answers in your notepad.

a. What are you happy to do for others?

b. What do you find yourself doing because you are compelled to, even though it may not be important or a priority?

c. What are you successful in?

d. Highlight any descriptive words that are similar in nature

Please feel free to choose any other scenario and follow the same process.

Step 5

Finding your genius question.

Look at all the words you have highlighted for similarities and common themes, and then do the following:

a. From all your highlighted words, choose only one or two that in your opinion feels as if it's the best fit

b. You now want to take these words and create a short question. You do this by beginning the question with 'How can I ...?' 'How do I ...?' 'What is...?' or similar words to that effect. For example, Gabrielle's question is, 'How can I make this more effective and efficient?' and David's question is 'What is the truth of this situation?'

c. See if this question feels right. If it does not, keep experimenting with different words until you find a question that feels right.

d. When you have found the question that feels right, test it in everyday scenarios – be it your work, home or social life – to see if it holds true in all situations. If it does then great, you have found your genius question.

e.   If it doesn't feel right just keep fine tuning the words. It may not be immediately evident; however, it is worth persevering and you will eventually get there.

Step 6

Uncovering your genius.

Once you have ascertained what your question is, the next step will be to uncover your genius. You do this by formulating an answer to the question you devised in Step 5. As stated before, your genius will take the form of an action process. It can be broken down as follows:

'I (insert verb) (insert noun).'

In the example of Gabrielle, her genius is, 'I create (*verb*) flow (*noun*).'

In the case of David, his genius is, 'I find (*verb*) the truth (*noun*).'

a.   Write the answer that best suits your question from Step 5 in the format above

b.   When you have found an answer that feels right, test it in everyday scenarios – be it your work, home or social life – to see if it holds true

c.   If it doesn't just keep thinking of answers to suit your question until you find a statement of your genius that feels right for you

d.   Again, it may not be immediately evident and, if not, just keep persevering

Step 7

Record your genius question and genius statement on your 'Results Page'.

Final Words

As you may have gathered this is not a linear process. It takes trial, error, intuition and time to really understand what your genius is. However, it is worth the effort as your genius will not only support you 100% in the work you were born to do but it makes it almost effortless for you.

> It takes trial, error, intuition and time to really understand what your genius is.

Many people may have the same training, qualification and experience in a particular field. But that does not necessarily mean that they are right for that profession. Unless your genius is suited to that job or profession, you will find it a challenge. This is why there are so many that struggle in their work environment. It is because their genius is not being utilised which means that they have to put extra energy and effort into their jobs, leaving them exhausted at the end of the day. It is only when the work you are doing is in alignment with your genius that you will soar. Not only will you find the process effortless but your energy levels will remain high because you are in your natural flow.

CHAPTER 9

WHO, WHAT AND WHERE

Introduction

In the previous chapters we looked at both the seen and unseen aspects of the work you were born to do. The unseen aspects are your Inner Codes™, Inherent Nature™ and Internal Process™ derived from your genius. These are the aspects that are often omitted from career guidance, courses or workshops that direct you to what you were born to do. However, as you may have gathered these unseen aspects are critical to ensuring your happiness and authenticity.

The seen or visible aspects of the work you were born to do are your talents and the activities that you are drawn to. These must be supported by the unseen aspects. There is only one area left on the visible aspects and that is for you to choose who you would like to work with, which sector that would fall in, and where and in which environment you would like to work.

Whatever it is you were born to do will be in the service of others. This is the purpose of all of humanity. We all have a duty to pay it forward by giving back to society. This ensures you play your part

> Whatever it is you were born to do will be in the service of others. This is the purpose of all of humanity.

in the evolution of mankind, leaving the world in a better place than you found it. When you are in the service of others your energy expands outwards, which is good for you, mankind and the planet.

In this section we will look at the final pieces of the puzzle.

Who would you most like to serve?

There are certain groups of people we are drawn to. In our workshops and training we primarily work with women. The people our clients choose to work with are varied, from young children to the elderly. Even if you choose to work within a certain sector of the population, for example, women, you may choose to work with a subset of that sector. For example, we work with women who are looking for their purpose in life. One of our clients, Suzanne, coaches women who wish to move up the career ladder.

Think about whether there is any sector of the population you are particularly drawn to. Here are a few examples to get you started:

- Consumers
- Students
- Children
- Elderly
- Sick

Once you have decided who you would most like to serve, record this on your 'Results Page'.

Which particular industry would you like to work in?

To a certain extent you should have a rough idea of the activities you are drawn to, based on the work you did in Chapter 3. This will give you some indication as to the industry that will be best suited to you. It may be that you would like to work within a certain niche in that industry. The choice is yours. Listed below are the main industries to get you started (please note that this is not a comprehensive list; you may want to research other areas). Choose the one that most resonates with you, either from the list or from your research.

- Sciences
- Information
- Technology
- Finance
- Health
- Healing
- Personal Development
- Spiritual Development
- Consumer Goods
- Media
- Arts

Once you have decided which industry and/or niche appeals to you, record it on your 'Results Page'.

Where would you like to work?

Your environment is very important to your health and well-being. It can either increase your energy or drain you. Refer to your Inner Codes™ to ensure that your environment does not impede them in any way. We are often expected to conform to the traditional (and sometimes inflexible and constricting) environments offered by the current job market. But the world is fast changing, and in this new age of

> Your environment is very important to your health and well-being. It can either increase your energy or drain you.

technological advances and instant communication you now have choices that were previously unavailable. You are no longer forced to work in the traditional office environment. The world is your oyster and you can use your imagination to decide what would be the most inspiring work environment for you.

Use the list below to get you started.

- Outdoors
- Indoors
- Global
- Specific country
- Specific climate

Once you have decided on the perfect work environment for you, record it on your 'Results Page'.

Final Words

The who, what and where is a matter of personal preference and these can change over time. But you need to start thinking about your choices a) to give you a starting point and something concrete to work towards and b) to help in the visualisation process that we will look at in the next chapter.

CHAPTER 10

THE WORK YOU WERE BORN TO DO

Introduction

Throughout the previous chapters and also in the section above you have been documenting the results of all the exercises onto your 'Results Page'. This page should now contain:

- Your top 5 Inner Codes™
- The shortlisted activities you are drawn to
- Whether you are an introvert or extrovert
- Your Preferred Representational System
- Your 9 Energetic Qualities and any related key-words
- Your talents
- Your Internal Process™ and Genius
- Who you would most like to serve
- Which industry or sector you are drawn to
- Where and in which environment you would like to work

The reason we have asked you to combine all the information that you have is to enable you to see it all in one place so that ideas and connections can form. We will talk about ideas in the next section but for now ensure that all the information listed above is on your 'Results Page'.

Your Born To Do Trigger Board

It would be worthwhile for you to invest in an A3 sized notice board or something similar to transfer the information from your 'Results Page'. This way you can be more creative in how you display the information. Doing this enables you to breathe life into these raw materials, creating links and triggering aha moments on the work you were born to do. We will call this your 'Born To Do Trigger Board'.

Creating your Born To Do Trigger Board masterpiece

Here are some suggestions to bring your masterpiece to life.

1. **Find images where possible to support the words.**

   Your mind tends to remember things much better in images rather than in words. So wherever you can get a pictorial representation of the words, please include these on the Trigger Board.

2. **Use different colours to bring your words to life.**

   We are naturally drawn to vibrant colours. In your Trigger Board use as many colours as you like to write words, draw images or highlight key-words.

3. **Include your favourite affirmations.**

   Affirmations are a very gentle way of breaking through any barriers of doubts, fears or insecurities. They are sentences that contain a positive action or attribute that is usually stated in the present tense. For example, if you often experience bouts of low self-esteem, your affirmation could be, 'I am strong, powerful and confident'. Or if you are doubtful of whether you will find what you were born to do, your affirmation may be, 'I live my purpose and I am doing what I was born to do'.

> Affirmations are a very gentle way of breaking through any barriers of doubts, fears or insecurities.

Affirmations need to be repeated as often as you can, whether in your mind or out loud in order for them to work their magic. Include any affirmations that would be helpful to you on your Trigger Board.

4. **Include your favourite quotes.**

   Inspirational quotes can shift your mindset or reframe your thoughts. They are wonderful tools to include on your Trigger Board to keep you inspired. For example, here is a beautiful quote by Ralph Waldo Emerson: 'What lies behind us and what lies ahead of us are tiny matters compared to what lies within us'; or Helen Keller's 'Life is either a great adventure or nothing'.

5. **Place it in a prominent place where you can see it often.**

   Remember, out of sight is out of mind so place your Trigger Board where you can see it frequently. The reasons for this are three-fold:

   a. Every time you look at the board an energetic connection is formed. This allows the information on the board to sink into your subconscious so that even though you may not be consciously looking for the answers, your unconscious mind is doing the work for you.

b. It keeps you focused on the task. There is a well-known saying that 'where attention goes, energy flows and results show'. The more you are focused on the task, the greater the chance you have of getting results. In addition, your innermost dominant thoughts become your outermost tangible reality. If you are constantly thinking about the work you were born to do with an end purpose it will start to move into reality. It is essential to focus on what you would love to be, do and have in life. Most people spend their time thinking about what they don't want as opposed to what they do want. And what happens is that the things they don't want continue to show up in their life. Your Trigger Board allows you to concentrate on the things you do want.

c. It may be viewed by others who can give an alternative perspective to help you come up with ideas that link the information on the board.

6. **Ask the question, 'What was I Born to Do?'**

This is perhaps the most important step. Asking is one of the most powerful, yet under-utilised tools for getting what you want. When your mind is confronted with a question it immediately sets about trying to find an answer. So when you are viewing your Trigger Board ask yourself (in your mind or out loud), *'Using all the information that is on the board, what was I was born to do?'* Your mind then starts to make connections and get ideas.

> Asking is one of the most powerful, yet under-utilised tools for getting what you want.

How ideas are created

Once you have put all your results onto your Born To Do Trigger Board in your own creative style, you can continue to add anything that you feel will inspire you. Now that all the elements are in your awareness, your mind will create associations and generate ideas. In order to help you with this process it would be helpful to know more about the concept of ideas and the journey required.

What are ideas?

Ideas are simply basic components and materials that are made into new combinations and relationships to produce a new outcome. There is a book called *A Technique for Producing Ideas* by James Webb Young. It helps you to outline the process for coming up with ideas and what to do with them. Here is a summary of the main steps:

STEP 1: Gather raw materials.

Most people wait around for inspiration to strike. If you are lucky it does but for the vast majority of us we need a little help. This help comes in the form of gathering the raw materials. This is normally quite a chore but thankfully you have already completed this via your Born To Do Trigger Board. This will be your focal point for generating ideas.

STEP 2: Work over these materials in your mind and ask relevant questions.

This aspect of generating ideas is the incubation stage where you allow your unconscious mind to make all the connections. Asking relevant questions at this stage is very helpful but you need to ask the right questions. In the Born To Do Trigger Board section above we suggested that you ask the question, *'Using all the information that is on the board, what was I was born to do?'* in suggestion 6. This is the most important question you can ask; however, you may ask any other questions should you feel inspired.

STEP 3: Out of nowhere the idea will appear.

In Step 2 you have been asking the questions and thinking of the answers, and this is your conscious mind at play. The answers or ideas usually come to you when you are least expecting it – while bathing, walking or it may wake you in the middle of the night. These are the times when you have switched your conscious mind off and your unconscious mind is allowed to surface. It usually happens when you don't have access to pen and paper, so make sure you have some way of recording your flashes of inspiration.

STEP 4: Take your newborn idea out into the world.

What we mean by this is whatever idea you come up with, you need to take some action. An idea without action will always remain an idea. What action you should take depends on the idea. You can research your ideas, talk to others, and ask for advice and direction, or perhaps look to others in the same area to understand their approach. Any of these will generate even more ideas that you can continue to explore.

STEP 5: Keep refining your ideas.

You may notice that not all your ideas will pan out. They are not all meant to. It is all part of the discovery process. The refining process means discarding those ideas that are no longer viable and moving forward with those that are taking you in the direction that you need to go in. The end point is to take the idea and follow it through so that you will eventually have a tangible product or service. Be patient, this may take time.

Final Words

If you think of the word synergy, this is where the sum of the whole is much more than the sum of the combined parts. It is almost like an invisible energy that infuses all the parts and brings it to life as a whole. This is what *Finding Your Truth and Discovering the Work You Were Born to Do* is all about. You have accumulated the parts in the previous chapters and put them together on your Born To Do Trigger Board so that synergy will occur as the ideas come to life.

> You need to trust the process. As with anything else, you need to be patient, disciplined and persistent.

This is a process like anything else. And if you follow the process through you will get more and more comfortable with it and you will see results at the end. You need to trust the process. As with anything else, you need to be patient, disciplined and persistent.

The final chapter will provide you with suggestions to keep the momentum going.

CHAPTER 11

WHERE DO YOU GO FROM HERE?

Introduction

In the previous chapters we have taken you through the entire process from start to finish, on how to find your truth and discover what you were born to do. This chapter gives you guidance on having the right mindset in order to keep the momentum going and what to expect along your journey.

Additionally, go to www.findingyourtruthbook.com to download three key bonus trainings that will help support you as you go through this final chapter.

The most frequently asked question

In our many workshops, coaching and mentoring sessions we are frequently asked: '*How long this process will take?*' This is usually due to the fact that most people are looking for a quick fix and instant solution to their problems. Because of this they are drawn to profiling tools and questions to try and get an insight into who they are. However,

> We are complex creatures shaped by nature, nurture and external influences, and no two people are alike.

the answers provided by these tools can sometimes be very generic, but more importantly they are incomplete. This is because we are complex creatures shaped by nature, nurture and external influences, and no two people are alike. The work you were born to do will be unique for each individual, but also the time taken to understand what you were born to do will also be unique to you. The final and very important note on this matter is that there is no end point for discovering the work you were born to do. It is an ongoing organic process and a constant evolution. When you step into what it is you were born to do a path is open to you and you cannot help wanting to continue on that path for as long as you possibly can.

Answering the question, 'How long will it take?'

The answer will depend on the following:

- **How well you know your true self**

  People who come to our workshops range from:

  ọ *Those who are approaching this topic for the very first time.*

  If you fall into this category you may not have done any previous work on yourself and the questions may appear strange to you. The questions have been specifically designed to help you think laterally and to gain a different perspective on yourself. It is advisable to repeat the exercises at least two to three times over a period of at least six months until there is clarity in the answers that you give and you are not second guessing yourself. If you fall into this category this may not be as quick a process as you would like it to be.

Ǫ *Those who have invested time and effort into courses or books. They have not yet found a satisfactory answer and are still searching.*

If you fall into this category it could be that the way the information was taught or presented to you was not compatible with your style or it failed to shed any light for you. As a result you did not get the answers you were looking for. If you fall into this category this may not be a quick process for you. This is because you may need to leave behind what you learnt to pave the way for the truth.

Ǫ *Those who have invested time and effort into courses or books. They have some of the relevant pieces of the puzzle but they have no idea of how to put them together to come up with a tangible, grounded solution.*

If you fall into this category you have done quite a bit of the groundwork already and you are definitely on your way. This book will both enhance and refine your previous efforts and you will find more things clicking into place as you progress. For you this will be a quicker process than the two categories stated above. In saying that, however, it will also depend on the very important factor noted below.

- **How much effort you put into the process.**

As with everything else your rate of success is directly proportional to the amount of time and energy invested in the process. The more focused effort you put into this journey, the greater the results.

> Your rate of success is directly proportional to the amount of time and energy invested in the process.

Therefore, asking, 'How long before this all falls into place' is like asking how long is a piece of string, and will depend on the two factors above.

You have completed the exercises in this book, so where do you go from here?

The best advice we can give you is to learn to live your life at cause and not at effect. What do we mean by that? To live your life at 'cause' is to live as if you were in control; either of what happens to you or of what you do with what happens to you. To live your life at 'effect' is to live your life as if you have no choice or say in how it turns out. Things just happen to you and you just accept it.

The majority of the population live their life at 'effect' and as such accept the status quo. Most successful people live at 'cause', challenging the status quo, shaping their destiny and knowing that their quality of life depends on the choices they make. You have made a life-changing decision by reading this book and completing the exercises within it. This action is a great start to you living your life at 'cause'.

As you continue your journey

Here are more suggestions to help you live at 'cause':

1. **Create time.**

   'Do not wait, the time will never be "just right". Start where you stand and work with whatever tools you may have at your command, and better tools will be found as you go along.' - Napoleon Hill, Author of *Think and Grow Rich*

   There is a tendency to wait for the 'right' time to begin. Some fail to carve out dedicated time to continue this journey of self-discovery. Both of these will stop you from moving forward. Determine where you want to be and put a strategy in place to get there. There is power in plans. Decide what you are going to achieve over the next month or two, or even further ahead. It could be researching your topic, taking a course or redoing the exercises for greater clarity. Get rid of a few things on your calendar so that you can devote more time to this. Whatever it is, plan it, write it and action it!

2. **Be determined.**

   This journey is about you finding your truth and what you were born to do. It is imperative that you remain focused and committed as this is the only path to true fulfilment. Transformational journeys are not always smooth sailing but they are definitely worth the ride. Be determined and never give up hope.

3. **Be courageous and have faith.**

   Don't be afraid to take the next step because you are unsure of the outcome. Every step is the right step. Every decision will lead to a learning and all learning contributes to growth. You can never be fully prepared for the unknown, otherwise it would not be the unknown. All human and personal advances come from a new step and an uncertain step. If you take too many precautions then you will never move forward. The worst that could happen is that you gain greater clarity that will bring you one step closer to finding work you were born to do.

Keeping the momentum going

If at any point you feel stuck along the journey or feel as if you are losing momentum use the following questions to help you get back on track:

1. **If you were to abandon this quest now where would you be in three years' time?**

2. **How do you feel about what you have just written?**

3. **What is getting in the way of you following your path?**

4. **How do you propose to resolve your answers to question 3?**

Create a plan to deal with your answers to question 4. Once you have resolved these issues this will clear the way for you to continue on your journey.

As you step into the truth of who you are here is what to expect

This journey is about transformational growth. As you step onto your path you will notice that you have a new way of thinking that will lead to profound changes. The following points outline those changes:

- **Your vibrational energy changes**.

  As you step into the truth of who you are and the work you were born to do your energetic vibration increases to a higher frequency. What this means for you is that you feel more connected to source. Things at a lower vibrational frequency that are not currently serving you will begin to fall away. These will be replaced with new circumstances and connections that match your new higher energetic signature.

  > when you step into your truth and begin to do the work you were born to do the Universe fully supports you.

- **You will start to tap into the power of the Universe.**

  When you are not on your path the Universe seldom supports you, which is why life seems to be a struggle and an uphill battle. However, when you step into your truth and begin to do the work you were born to do the Universe fully supports you. This means that you will find new opportunities opening to you, the law of attraction is at its most powerful and answers come to you more readily.

- **Your confidence grows.**

  As with anything, the more you step into it and own it, the more confident you become. Whatever you were born to do will come to you naturally because it is who you are at your core. When you step into this power you will gain confidence, not just in what you were born to do but also in other areas needed to propel you forward.

- **You will notice accelerated growth.**

  This happens as a result of the convergence of all three points noted above. Higher energetic frequency, the ability to tap into the power of the Universe and increased confidence all ensure that your life moves ahead at an accelerated rate.

- **You will begin to achieve total congruency.**

  Total congruency is living your life in alignment with the essence of who you are. You remain the same whether you are alone, with family, with friends or at work. This book is about understanding the core of who you are and what you were born to do. If you ensure your Inner Codes™ are being supported, do what you love, use your natural talents and head towards your ultimate vision, then you will have achieved total congruency in what you are about. This is the end goal.

Your journey has just begun

'The one thing all famous authors, world-class athletes, business tycoons, singers, actors and celebrated achievers in any field have in common is that they all began their journey when they were none of these. Yet still, they began their journey.' - Mike Dooley

You have begun your journey in a very profound way and we wish you every success as you move forward.

APPENDICES

APPENDIX 1

INNER CODES™

➤ Accomplishment	➤ Environment	➤ Mastery
➤ Achievement	➤ Freedom	➤ Nurture
➤ Acknowledgement	➤ Fulfilment	➤ Openness
➤ Adventure	➤ Fun	➤ Orderliness
➤ Balance	➤ Health	➤ Organisation
➤ Clarity	➤ Honesty	➤ Personal power
➤ Commitment	➤ Humour	➤ Recognition
➤ Community	➤ Independence	➤ Risk taking
➤ Compassion	➤ Integrity	➤ Security
➤ Completion	➤ Joy	➤ Self-expression
➤ Connection	➤ Leadership	➤ Service
➤ Creativity	➤ Learning	➤ Spirituality
➤ Emotional Health	➤ Magic	➤ Trust

APPENDIX 2

KEY AREAS AND TRANSITIONS IN YOUR LIFE

The 8 Different Areas of Life

➤ Physical	➤ Partner
➤ Spiritual	➤ Family
➤ Mental	➤ Finances
➤ Career	➤ Social

Chronological Sequence of Your Life

3 – 5 ► Kindergarten

5 – 11 ► Primary School

12 – 18 ► Secondary School

18 – 23 ► Higher Education (if applicable)

23 onwards ► Various Jobs in Chronological Order

APPENDIX 3

INNER CODES™ GRID

INNER CODE	1	2	3	4	5	6	7	8	TOTAL
Accomplishment									
Achievement									
Acknowledgement									
Adventure									
Balance									
Clarity									
Commitment									
Community									
Compassion									
Completion									
Connection									
Creativity									
Emotional Health									
Environment									
Freedom									
Fulfilment									
Fun									
Health									
Honesty									
Humour									
Independence									
Integrity									
Joy									
Leadership									
Learning									
Magic									
Mastery									
Nurture									
Openness									
Orderliness									
Organisation									
Personal Power									
Recognition									
Risk Taking									
Security									
Self-expression									
Service									
Spirituality									
Trust									

APPENDIX 4

TOP 5 INNER CODES™

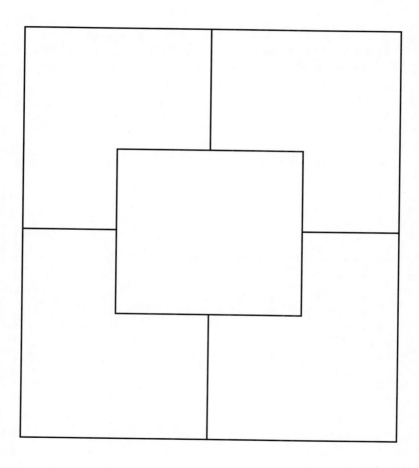

ACTIVITIES YOU ARE DRAWN TO

Column 1	Column 2	Column 3	Column 4

Column 1	Column 2	Column 3	Column 4

Column 1	Column 2	Column 3	Column 4

Column 1	Column 2	Column 3	Column 4

Column 1	Column 2	Column 3	Column 4

Column 1	Column 2	Column 3	Column 4

Column 1	Column 2	Column 3	Column 4

Column 1	Column 2	Column 3	Column 4

Column 1	Column 2	Column 3	Column 4

Column 1	Column 2	Column 3	Column 4

APPENDIX 6

ARE YOU AN INTROVERT, EXTROVERT OR JUST PLAIN SHY?

Extrovert	**Y/N**
You are energised by people.	
You dislike and become bored being alone.	
You like to talk about yourself or be the centre of attention.	
You enjoy talking about anything and everything with anyone.	
You speak to fill silence, even if you have nothing particularly important to say.	
You like to have verbal brainstorms to help you formulate your thoughts.	
Total number of 'Yes'	

Introvert	**Y/N**
Being around people can be draining.	
After being around people, you enjoy solitude to contemplate.	
You like to listen to others and consider what they said before responding.	
You dislike small talk and speaking with strangers with no purpose in mind.	

You will speak when you think it is necessary to make a point.	
It is much easier to formulate your thoughts while writing or when alone.	
Total number of 'Yes'	

Shy	Y/N
You are anxious or nervous around people.	
You avoid social situations.	
You speak only when necessary.	
You have a difficult time talking to acquaintances or strangers.	
You avoid speaking unless you are with one of your very close friends.	
You hope you are not required to verbalise your thoughts.	
Total number of 'Yes'	

WHAT IS YOUR PREFERRED REPRESENTATIONAL SYSTEM: ASSESSMENT

People tend to use one representational system over another.

This becomes their Preferred or Primary Representational System.

For each of the following statements, please place a number next to every phrase.

4 ➤ Almost always

3 ➤ Often

2 ➤ Sometimes

1 ➤ Almost never

1. I make a choice when:

_____ It feels right to me

_____ I hear it and it sounds right to me

_____ I see it and it looks great

_____ I review it and it fits my criteria

2. When discussing an issue, I am persuaded by:

_____ how convincing the other person sounds

_____ really seeing the other's point of view

_____ how reasonable the individual makes the point

_____ my own gut feeling

3. When I meet someone for the first time, I am impressed by:

    _____ the appearance of the person

    _____ how he or she makes me feel

    _____ how articulate or intelligent the individual is

    _____ if what the person says rings true to me

4. I generally respond to:

    _____ sounds, and I am easily distracted by noises

    _____ interesting facts, and I am easily distracted by my own thoughts

    _____ sensations, and I am easily distracted by the way my body feels

    _____ colours, and I am easily distracted by sights around me

5. When I like a proposal, I tend to say things like:

    _____ 'Sounds good'

    _____ 'Makes sense'

    _____ 'Got it'

    _____ 'Looks good'

APPENDIX 8

WHAT IS YOUR PREFERRED REPRESENTATIONAL SYSTEM: RESULTS

Step 1:

Copy the numbers values from the assessment page in exactly the same sequence you wrote them.

Q1	Q2	Q3	Q4	Q5
_____K	_____A	_____V	_____A	_____A
_____A	_____V	_____K	_____Ad	_____Ad
_____V	_____Ad	_____Ad	_____K	_____K
_____Ad	_____K	_____A	_____V	_____V

Step 2:

Record the values assigned to each letter in Step 1 for the 5 questions in the columns below. Then total each column. For example, record the 'V' values for all 5 questions in column 1 and total that column. Repeat for columns A, K and Ad.

	V	A	K	Ad
Q1				
Q2				
Q3				
Q4				
Q5				
TOTAL				

Step 3:

The scores in each column will give the relative preference for each of the four major Representational Systems. The highest total will be your Preferred Representational System.

From "Christopher Howard Results Certification Course"

APPENDIX 9

9 ENERGETIC QUALITIES CALCULATIONS

Step 1

Complete Year Chart (1910 – 2017)

F	6	7	8	9	1	2	3	4	5
M	9	8	7	6	5	4	3	2	1
	1910 (feb 5th)	1911 (feb 5th)	1912 (feb 5th)	1913 (feb 4th)	1914 (feb 5th)	1915 (feb 5th)	1916 (feb 5th)	1917 (feb 4th)	1918 (feb 5th)
	1919 (feb 5th)	1920 (feb 5th)	1921 (feb 4th)	1922 (feb 5th)	1923 (feb 5th)	1924 (feb 5th)	1925 (feb 4th)	1926 (feb 4th)	1927 (feb 5th)
	1928 (feb 5th)	1929 (feb 4th)	1930 (feb 4th)	1931 (feb 5th)	1932 (feb 5th)	1933 (feb 4th)	1934 (feb 4th)	1935 (feb 4th)	1936 (feb 5th)
	1937 (feb 4th)	1938 (feb 4th)	1939 (feb 5th)	1940 (feb 5th)	1941 (feb 4th)	1942 (feb 4th)	1943 (feb 5th)	1944 (feb 5th)	1945 (feb 4th)
	1946 (feb 4th)	1947 (feb 5th)	1948 (feb 5th)	1949 (feb 4th)	1950 (feb 4th)	1951 (feb 5th)	1952 (feb 5th)	1953 (feb 4th)	1954 (feb 4th)
	1955 (feb 5th)	1956 (feb 5th)	1957 (feb 4th)	1958 (feb 4th)	1959 (feb 4th)	1960 (feb 5th)	1961 (feb 4th)	1962 (feb 4th)	1963 (feb 4th)
	1964 (feb 5th)	1965 (feb 4th)	1966 (feb 4th)	1967 (feb 4th)	1968 (feb 5th)	1969 (feb 4th)	1970 (feb 4th)	1971 (feb 4th)	1972 (feb 5th)
	1973 (feb 4th)	1974 (feb 4th)	1975 (feb 4th)	1976 (feb 5th)	1977 (feb 4th)	1978 (feb 4th)	1979 (feb 4th)	1980 (feb 5th)	1981 (feb 4th)
	1982 (feb 4th)	1983 (feb 4th)	1984 (feb 4th)	1985 (feb 4th)	1986 (feb 4th)	1987 (feb 4th)	1988 (feb 4th)	1989 (feb 4th)	1990 (feb 4th)
	1991 (feb 4th)	1992 (feb 4th)	1993 (feb 4th)	1994 (feb 4th)	1995 (feb 4th)	1996 (feb 4th)	1997 (feb 4th)	1998 (feb 4th)	1999 (feb 4th)
	2000 (feb 4th)	2001 (feb 5th)	2002 (feb 4th)	2003 (feb 4th)	2004 (feb 4th)	2005 (feb 5th)	2006 (feb 5th)	2007 (feb 4th)	2008 (feb 4th)
	2009 (feb 5th)	2010 (feb 4th)	2011 (feb 4th)	2012 (feb 4th)	2013 (feb 4th)	2014 (feb 4th)	2015 (feb 4th)	2016 (feb 4th)	2017 (feb 4th)

- *February 4th is the key date. The above shows some dates as Feb 4th, others as Feb 5th. Please, use a more instinctive sense about the personality to ascertain if a person is the year before or after, if they are close to Feb 4th or 5th, and especially if they are from a different time zone.*

Step 2

For 1, 4 and 7 Years

	F	M	A	M	J	J	A	S	O	N	D	J
MALE	8	7	6	5	4	3	2	1	9	8	7	6
FEMALE	7	8	9	1	2	3	4	5	6	7	8	9

For 3, 6 and 9 Years

	F	M	A	M	J	J	A	S	O	N	D	J
MALE	5	4	3	2	1	9	8	7	6	5	4	3
FEMALE	1	2	3	4	5	6	7	8	9	1	2	3

For 2, 5 and 8 Years

	F	M	A	M	J	J	A	S	O	N	D	J
MALE	2	1	9	8	7	6	5	4	3	2	1	9
FEMALE	4	5	6	7	8	9	1	2	3	4	5	6

Step 3

YEAR → MONTH ↓	1	2	3	4	5	6	7	8	9
1	1-1-5	2-1-6	3-1-7	4-1-8	5-1-9	6-1-1	7-1-2	8-1-3	9-1-4
2	1-2-4	2-2-5	3-2-6	4-2-7	5-2-8	6-2-9	7-2-1	8-2-2	9-2-3
3	1-3-3	2-3-4	3-3-5	4-3-6	5-3-7	6-3-8	7-3-9	8-3-1	9-3-2
4	1-4-2	2-4-3	3-4-4	4-4-5	5-4-6	6-4-7	7-4-8	8-4-9	9-4-1
5	1-5-1	2-5-2	3-5-3	4-5-4	5-5-5	6-5-6	7-5-7	8-5-8	9-5-9
6	1-6-9	2-6-1	3-6-2	4-6-3	5-6-4	6-6-5	7-6-6	8-6-7	9-6-8
7	1-7-8	2-7-9	3-7-1	4-7-2	5-7-3	6-7-4	7-7-5	8-7-6	9-7-7
8	1-8-7	2-8-8	3-8-9	2-8-2	5-8-2	6-8-3	7-8-4	8-8-5	9-8-6
9	1-9-6	2-9-7	3-9-8	4-9-9	5-9-1	6-9-2	7-9-3	8-9-4	9-9-5

ABOUT THE AUTHORS

Michele Yeomans
International Speaker, Educator, Mentor

After 30 years as a successful accountant and entrepreneur, Michele realised her true vocation and embarked on an exciting new career path. A sought-after international speaker, educator and mentor, she has co-developed programmes and strategies, built upon her professional achievements, personal insights and intuitive wisdom to help others become the best they can be.

Her natural talent for empowering those around her, coupled with her innate ability to channel her energy for a higher purpose, inspires Michele to strive to help people find their inner happiness and ultimate fulfilment, teaching them how to relax into life and navigate through conflicts with ease. She works to help others discover the work that they were born to do, understand their purpose and assist them to unearth their potential to awaken their true self – all of which she has experienced herself in her own journey of healing.

Michele speaks frequently at major conferences and has shared stages with Dame DC Cordova, CEO of the global organisation, 'Money and You'; and Laura Tenison, founder of JoJo Maman Bébé. She has also been featured on Voice America and Croydon Radio. She is the co-founder of Living

The True Self, a company dedicated to showing the path to a truly authentic life.

Mala Bridgelal Ram
Educator, Intuitive Healer and Truth Seeker

After 17 years in the Healthcare Industry and frustrated by the bureaucracy and shortcomings of the healthcare system, Mala chose to pursue her own path in health and healing. With her understanding that the cause of ill health is not limited to the physical, she is a true healer working not only on the physical but also on the emotional and spiritual, and has co-developed workshops and programmes to support this.

Mala is an intuitive healer and natural psychologist who has a passion for grasping the underlying nature of human behaviour. Drawing from her experience in nursing, she works with individuals, helping them to clear their physical and emotional blocks so that they can move forward and have the happiness they deserve. Because her healing is very intuitive-based she operates through a unique combination, drawing upon the combined practices of craniosacral work, and energy and sound healing. With this approach she allows, teaches and enables the client to heal and self-heal in a very relaxed and caring manner.

Mala has been involved in international projects that challenge the status quo of the healthcare system and she is also the co-founder of Living the True Self, a company dedicated to showing the path to a truly authentic life.

ADDITIONAL COURSES AND WORKSHOPS

In addition to *Discover the Work You Were Born to Do*, the other programmes in our foundation level include:

- Building Your Emotional Resilience – Here we explore the emotions that are holding you back. Learn how to handle and diffuse them so that you can move towards a more centred and calm frame of mind.

- Your Route to Vibrant Health – Learn how to heal yourself and intuitively manage your health so that you have more choice and control over your day to day well-being.

- Creating Harmony in Your Relationships – Learn how to communicate with and understand others so that you can take your relationships to a whole new level.

These are available as live workshops and digital courses.